# All About Witnessing

## A Study of the Book of Acts

outreach

# All About Witnessing

## A Study of the Book of Acts



Robert J. Martin

BAKER BOOK HOUSE
Grand Rapids, Michigan

ISBN: 0-8010-5970-4
Printed in the United States of America

to
EMERSON WARD
and
CARLYLE GINTER
two outstanding
twentieth-century witnesses
and to
MARTHA MINER
and
CHARLES R. HEMBREE
who stimulated and encouraged me
to share my thoughts with
other witnesses

## *CONTENTS*

### PREPARING THE WITNESSES (1:1-26)



### PHASE ONE: WITNESSING IN JERUSALEM (2:1–7:60)



### PHASE TWO: WITNESSING IN JUDAEA AND SAMARIA (8:1–12:25)



### PHASE THREE: WITNESSING IN THE GENTILE WORLD (13:1–28:31)

# INTRODUCTION

Has witnessing ever been a problem to you? Are you troubled because you feel you are not witnessing for Jesus Christ as you should? Would you like some sound advice on your problem?

When we have a problem with our health or our automobiles, we go to an expert for some advice and/or remedy. And we allow the expert to do most or all of the talking. We defer to his judgment on ways to solve the problem.

No true Christian wants to be an inactive witness. So, let's go to the expert on witnessing, the Holy Spirit. He's given many directions and guidelines for witnesses and witnessing in the Book of Acts. He tells what witnessing is (and what it isn't), when to witness, and how to witness. Those who truly seek to learn will find that the Holy Spirit has a way of infusing them too with the enthusiasm, boldness, and excitement of the first-century witnesses. Such Spirit-controlled witnesses will begin to change their corner of the world first and then go on to turn a twentieth-century world upside down.

This is a discussion guide. No pat answers are given. Few comments are made. A host of questions are posed. This format is intended to make the user himself dig into Scripture and, with the guidance of the Holy Spirit, to come up with answers to questions about witnessing. The best way to use this book is in a group situation where people offer different insights and evaluations while inspiring each other to stretch their witnessing potential.

## *SUGGESTIONS FOR GROUP DISCUSSION*

Each member of the group should read the Book of Acts through several times before the discussion series on ALL ABOUT WITNESSING begins and continue reading the complete book through even though the discussion topic for the class may center on only a few verses of a given chapter.

Different versions of the Book of Acts may shed additional light on a given passage.

Especially the group leader, but also the participants, would benefit from using these study aids: *The New Testament from Twenty-six Translations; Young's Analytical Concordance to the Bible,* or *Cruden's Unabridged Concordance.*

Each member of the group should be invited to express opinions and raise questions. One way to involve everyone is to go around the circle, asking each member in turn to answer the next question. This has the added advantage of having each member prepare on every question because he won't know which question he'll be asked to answer.

At the end of each discussion period, the leader should sum up the lessons learned from that Scripture portion as they apply to witnesses and witnessing today.

Participants may wish to keep a notebook record on insights and lessons learned from each discussion session. Another interesting practice is to keep a scrapbook of articles and pictures that deal with twentieth-century witnessing experiences.

# *PREPARING THE WITNESS (1:1-26)*

## 1. BEFORE CHRIST'S ASCENSION (1:1-8)

THE former treatise have I made, O Thē-ŏph′-ĭ-lŭs, of all that Jesus began both to do and teach,

2 Until the day in which he was taken up, after that he through the Holy Ghost had given commandments unto the apostles whom he had chosen:

3 To whom also he shewed himself alive after his passion by many infallible proofs, being seen of them forty days, and speaking of the things pertaining to the kingdom of God:

4 And, being assembled together with *them*, commanded them that they should not depart from Jerusalem, but wait for the promise of the Father, which, *saith he*, ye have heard of me.

5 For John truly baptized with water; but ye shall be baptized with the Holy Ghost not many days hence.

6 When they therefore were come together, they asked of him, saying, Lord, wilt thou at this time restore again the kingdom to Israel?

7 And he said unto them, It is not for you to know the times or the seasons, which the Father hath put in his own power.

8 But ye shall receive power, after that the Holy Ghost is come upon you: and ye shall be witnesses unto me both in Jerusalem, and in all Judæa, and in Samaria, and unto the uttermost part of the earth.

Some scholars have called this letter to Theophilus, Luke Two. Which of the following titles do you believe best expresses the theme of the letter?

Acts
The Acts of the Apostles
Acts of Jesus Christ Continued
A Church Is Born
Acts of the Witnesses
The Acts of Jesus Christ Through His Witnesses Empowered by the Holy Spirit

Compare the above passage with Luke 24:44-53. Are there any similarities? What light does the passage from Luke shed on Acts 1:1-9?

Read verse 8 again. Would you agree that this is the key

verse to the Book of Acts? Why, or why not? Can you see an outline for the whole Book of Acts in this verse? If so, what would the outline be?

Jot down several themes that you see in the Book of Acts. Is "witness" the central theme or subject? How many times does the word *witness* or its equivalent appear in Acts?

Is verse 8 a promise or a prophecy? What is the difference between the two?

What would you say a witness is?

What is the difference between a witness and witnessing?

Which of the following definitions of witnessing do you think is best:

1 Telling what one knows about a person or subject
2 Preaching
3 Testifying
4 One beggar telling another beggar where to find bread
5 Telling what one remembers of a thing he actually saw or experienced
6 Letting one's light shine
7 Doing good works

Which of these definitions best describes the work of the "witnesses" in verse 8?

What is the difference between the witnessing encounters of the disciples as recorded in the Gospels and what they preached and taught as recorded in Acts? (Compare Luke 9:1; 18-22 and 21:12-15 with Luke 10:1-9.)

Why were the disciples instructed to wait before they began to witness?

Compare Christ's words in Acts 1:8 with passages in John 14:16-26; 25:26-27; 16:7-14. Why was the Holy Spirit coming to the disciples? What effect would His coming have on their witnessing?

Who were they to be witnesses for or of? Why did they need the Holy Spirit to testify of Him? Did they need anything else beside the Holy Spirit to witness?

What was Christ's program schedule for the witnesses? Is that schedule still in effect today? Why, do you suppose, so many Christians are still waiting to witness? What percentage of Christians never witness?

Which of the following words are synonymous with *witnessing* in Acts: (It is best to look up the words in a *Strong's* or *Young's Concordance* because there the Greek word is defined and cross references are given)

| | |
|---|---|
| testify | tell |
| preach | speak |
| report | gospel |

They were to wait for power. Why? Who was included in the word *"they"?* From where was the power to come? Do we need to wait for power?

## 2. AFTER CHRIST'S ASCENSION (1:9-26)

9 And when he had spoken these things, while they beheld, he was taken up; and a cloud received him out of their sight.

10 And while they looked stedfastly toward heaven as he went up, behold, two men stood by them in white apparel;

11 Which also said, Ye men of Galilee, why stand ye gazing up into heaven? this same Jesus, which is taken up from you into heaven, shall so come in like manner as ye have seen him go into heaven.

12 Then returned they unto Jerusalem from the mount called Ŏl′-ĭ-vĕt, which is from Jerusalem a sabbath day's journey.

13 And when they were come in, they went up into an upper room, where abode both Peter, and James, and John, and Andrew, Philip, and Thomas, Bartholomew, and Matthew, James *the son* of Ăl-phǣ′-ŭs, and Simon Zē-lō′-tēs, and Judas *the brother* of James.

14 These all continued with one accord in prayer and supplication, with the women, and Mary the mother of Jesus, and with his brethren.

15 ¶ And in those days Peter stood up in the midst of the disciples, and said, (the number of names together were about an hundred and twenty,)

16 Men *and* brethren, this scripture must needs have been fulfilled, which the Holy Ghost by the mouth of David spake before concerning Judas, which was guide to them that took Jesus.

17 For he was numbered with us, and had obtained part of this ministry.

18 Now this man purchased a field with the reward of iniquity; and falling headlong, he burst asunder in the midst, and all his bowels gushed out.

19 And it was known unto all the dwellers at Jerusalem; insomuch as that field is called in their proper tongue, Ă-çĕl′-dă-mă, that is to say, The field of blood.

20 For it is written in the book of Psalms, Let his habitation be desolate, and let no man dwell therein: and his bishopric let another take.

21 Wherefore of these men which have companied with us all the time that the Lord Jesus went in and out among us,

22 Beginning from the baptism of John, unto that same day that he was taken up from us, must one be ordained to be a witness with us of his resurrection.

23 And they appointed two, Joseph called Băr′-să-băs, who was surnamed Justus, and Matthias.

24 And they prayed, and said, Thou, Lord, which knowest the hearts of all *men*, shew whether of these two thou hast chosen,

25 That he may take part of this ministry and apostleship, from which Judas by transgression fell, that he might go to his own place.

26 And they gave forth their lots; and the lot fell upon Matthias; and he was numbered with the eleven apostles.

Describe the events of Acts 1:10-26.

What does it mean to be of "one accord [mind]"? How many times is this phrase mentioned in Acts? In the New Testament? Look up the references given in a concordance and notice the context of each. Why is "being of one accord [mind]" an important factor in a church's witness?

What is the difference between prayer and supplication? Why is prayer important to the witness?

Were the disciples that gathered together saved? Did the disciples already possess the Holy Spirit (see John 20:22)?

Should a twentieth-century believer wait before witnessing? If so, why should he wait–and how long? Look for clues as you read through Acts again.

What are the qualifications of a witness?

List the people (excluding the apostles) in Acts who witnessed. The words *disciples* and *apostles* are used several times in the Book of Acts. What is the difference between these two words?

## *PHASE ONE: WITNESSING IN JERUSALEM (2:1–7:60)*

# 3. WITNESSING BY PREACHING (2:1-47)

AND when the day of Pentecost was fully come, they were all with one accord in one place.

2 And suddenly there came a sound from heaven as of a rushing mighty wind, and it filled all the house where they were sitting.

3 And there appeared unto them cloven tongues like as of fire, and it sat upon each of them.

4 And they were all filled with the Holy Ghost, and began to speak with other tongues, as the Spirit gave them utterance.

5 And there were dwelling at Jerusalem Jews, devout men, out of every nation under heaven.

6 Now when this was noised abroad, the multitude came together, and were confounded, because that every man heard them speak in his own language.

7 And they were all amazed and marvelled, saying one to another, Behold, are not all these which speak Galilæans?

8 And how hear we every man in our own tongue, wherein we were born?

9 Pär′-thĭ-ăns, and Medes, and Elamites, and the dwellers in Mĕs-ŏ-pŏ-tā′-mĭ-ă, and in Judæa, and Căp-pă-dō′-çĭ-ă, in Pontus, and Asia,

10 Phrygia, and Păm-phȳl′-ĭ-ă, in Egypt, and in the parts of Libya about Çȳ-rē′-nē, and strangers of Rome, Jews and proselytes,

11 Cretes and Arabians, we do hear them speak in our tongues the wonderful works of God.

12 And they were all amazed, and were in doubt, saying one to another, What meaneth this?

13 Others mocking said, These men are full of new wine.

14 ¶ But Peter, standing up with the eleven, lifted up his voice, and said unto them, Ye men of Judæa, and all *ye* that dwell at Jerusalem, be this known unto you, and hearken to my words:

15 For these are not drunken, as ye suppose, seeing it is *but* the third hour of the day.

16 But this is that which was spoken by the prophet Joel;

17 And it shall come to pass in the last days, saith God, I will pour out of my Spirit upon all flesh: and your sons and your daughters shall prophesy, and your young men shall see visions, and your old men shall dream dreams:

18 And on my servants and on my handmaidens I will pour out in those days of my Spirit; and they shall prophesy:

19 And I will shew wonders in heaven above, and signs in the earth beneath; blood, and fire, and vapour of smoke:

20 The sun shall be turned into darkness, and the moon into blood, before that great and notable day of the Lord come:

21 And it shall come to pass, *that* whosoever shall call on the name of the Lord shall be saved.

22 Ye men of Israel, hear these words; Jesus of Nazareth, a man approved of God among you by miracles and wonders and signs, which God did by him in the midst of you, as ye yourselves also know:

23 Him, being delivered by the determinate counsel and foreknowledge of God, ye have taken, and by wicked hands have crucified and slain:

24 Whom God hath raised up, having loosed the pains of death: because it was not possible that he should be holden of it.

25 For David speaketh concerning him, I foresaw the Lord always before my face, for he is on my right hand, that I should not be moved:

26 Therefore did my heart rejoice, and my tongue was glad; moreover also my flesh shall rest in hope:

27 Because thou wilt not leave my soul in hell, neither wilt thou suffer thine Holy One to see corruption.

28 Thou hast made known to me the ways of life; thou shalt make me full of joy with thy countenance.

29 Men *and* brethren, let me freely speak unto you of the patriarch David, that he is both dead and buried, and his sepulchre is with us unto this day.

30 Therefore being a prophet, and knowing that God had sworn with an oath to him, that of the fruit of his loins, according to the flesh, he would raise up Christ to sit on his throne;

31 He seeing this before spake of the resurrection of Christ, that his soul was not left in hell, neither his flesh did see corruption.

32 This Jesus hath God raised up, whereof we all are witnesses.

33 Therefore being by the right hand of God exalted, and having received of the Father the promise of the Holy Ghost, he hath shed forth this, which ye now see and hear.

34 For David is not ascended into the heavens: but he saith himself, The LORD said unto my Lord, Sit thou on my right hand,

35 Until I make thy foes thy footstool.

36 Therefore let all the house of Israel know assuredly, that God hath made that same Jesus, whom ye have crucified, both Lord and Christ.

37 ¶ Now when they heard *this*, they were pricked in their heart, and said unto Peter and to the rest of the apostles, Men *and* brethren, what shall we do?

38 Then Peter said unto them, Repent, and be baptized every one of you in the name of Jesus Christ for the remission of sins, and ye shall receive the gift of the Holy Ghost.

39 For the promise is unto you, and to your children, and to all that are afar off, *even* as many as the Lord our God shall call.

40 And with many other words did he testify and exhort, saying, Save yourselves from this untoward generation.

41 ¶ Then they that gladly received his word were baptized: and the same day there were added *unto them* about three thousand souls.

42 And they continued stedfastly in the apostles' doctrine and fellowship, and in breaking of bread, and in prayers.

43 And fear came upon every soul: and many wonders and signs were done by the apostles.

44 And all that believed were together, and had all things common;

45 And sold their possessions and goods, and parted them to all *men*, as every man had need.

46 And they, continuing daily with one accord in the temple, and breaking bread from house to house, did eat their meat with gladness and singleness of heart,

47 Praising God, and having favour with all the people. And the Lord added to the church daily such as should be saved.

Discuss the practical reasons why the Day of Pentecost was a good day to begin witnessing. (You may want to consult a good commentary.)

How could people from at least sixteen countries understand these witnesses from Galilee? What did God provide to meet this problem? (Give other examples from Acts that show how God *always* met *every* need of the witness.)

Compare the events surrounding the coming of Christ with those that surrounded the coming of the Holy Spirit. List the purposes of the comings. How were the purposes alike? How did they differ?

Notice how many times the phrase, "filled with the Holy Spirit," occurs in Acts. What always follows each special filling?

Discuss the words *filling, indwelling,* and *baptism* in relationship to the Holy Spirit. Define each. Are they separate or syronymous acts?

Peter's first words as a witness are recorded in verses 14-40. For a definition and illustration of a gospel message read I Corinthians 15:1-9 and Romans 10:9, 10. Point out at least four characteristics that make Peter's words a good witnessing message. As you read through Acts again notice whether or not the gospel is given with every verbal witness.

How many times is Christ's resurrection referred to in the Book of Acts? Why is His resurrection important? Is it always mentioned in connection with a witnessing opportunity? Think back to a witnessing experience you remember. Did your witness include the gospel? Did you emphasize the resurrected Lord?

Which of the following words best describe Peter's first witnessing attempt:

| | | |
|---|---|---|
| direct | honest | bold |
| antagonistic | bigoted | blunt |
| sincere | cruel | loving |
| necessary | overbearing | |

Add your own words of description.

Notice the response of the people to this first witnessing experience. How concerned should the witness be with the results?

Characterize the early church (the group of witnesses). What do these characteristics have to do with witnessing? Which is witnessing—living or telling? Why does it matter how the witness lives?

Who organized this first witnessing opportunity (Mark 16:20)? Isn't this great news for the witness?

Do you ever long for a spontaneous Spirit-filled, Christ-controlled witness experience?

## 4. WITNESSING BY MIRACLES (3:1-26)

NOW Peter and John went up together into the temple at the hour of prayer, *being* the ninth *hour*.

2 And a certain man lame from his mother's womb was carried, whom they laid daily at the gate of the temple which is called Beautiful, to ask alms of them that entered into the temple;

3 Who seeing Peter and John about to go into the temple asked an alms.

4 And Peter, fastening his eyes upon him with John, said, Look on us.

5 And he gave heed unto them, expecting to receive something of them.

6 Then Peter said, Silver and gold have I none; but such as I have give I thee: In the name of Jesus Christ of Nazareth rise up and walk.

7 And he took him by the right hand, and lifted *him* up: and immediately his feet and ankle bones received strength.

8 And he leaping up stood, and walked, and entered with them into the temple, walking, and leaping, and praising God.

9 And all the people saw him walking and praising God:

10 And they knew that it was he which sat for alms at the Beautiful gate of the temple: and they were filled with wonder and amazement at that which had happened unto him.

11 And as the lame man which was healed held Peter and John, all the people ran together unto them in the porch that is called Solomon's, greatly wondering.

12 ¶ And when Peter saw *it*, he answered unto the people, Ye men of Israel, why marvel ye at this? or why look ye so earnestly on us, as though by our own power or holiness we had made this man to walk?

13 The God of Abraham, and of Isaac, and of Jacob, the God of our fathers, hath glorified his Son Jesus; whom ye delivered up, and

denied him in the presence of Pilate, when he was determined to let *him* go.

14 But ye denied the Holy One and the Just, and desired a murderer to be granted unto you;

15 And killed the Prince of life, whom God hath raised from the dead; whereof we are witnesses.

16 And his name through faith in his name hath made this man strong, whom ye see and know: yea, the faith which is by him hath given him this perfect soundness in the presence of you all.

17 And now, brethren, I wot that through ignorance ye did *it*, as *did* also your rulers.

18 But those things, which God before had shewed by the mouth of all his prophets, that Christ should suffer, he hath so fulfilled.

19 ¶ Repent ye therefore, and be converted, that your sins may be blotted out, when the times of refreshing shall come from the presence of the Lord;

20 And he shall send Jesus Christ, which before was preached unto you:

21 Whom the heaven must receive until the times of restitution of all things, which God hath spoken by the mouth of all his holy prophets since the world began.

22 For Moses truly said unto the fathers, A prophet shall the Lord your God raise up unto you of your brethren, like unto me; him shall ye hear in all things whatsoever he shall say unto you.

23 And it shall come to pass, *that* every soul, which will not hear that prophet, shall be destroyed from among the people.

24 Yea, and all the prophets from Samuel and those that follow after, as many as have spoken, have likewise foretold of these days.

25 Ye are the children of the prophets, and of the covenant which God made with our fathers, saying unto Abraham, And in thy seed shall all the kindreds of the earth be blessed.

26 Unto you first God, having raised up his Son Jesus, sent him to bless you, in turning away every one of you from his iniquities.

Describe what happened as Peter and John were on their way to the temple for prayer. Why is prayer important to the witness? Was Peter's and John's first responsibility to witness or pray?

Give examples of how we can become too busy doing good things to witness. Could tradition have kept Peter and John from witnessing? Can you think of Christian traditions that might cause a believer to miss a witnessing opportunity?

What did the lame man think he needed? What did he really need? Do all men have this same basic need? How is this an advantage to witnessing?

Occasionally witnesses may have the opportunity to receive praise from men. How did Peter and John react to this praise?

All through the Book of Acts mighty miracles are recorded. Why were signs, wonders, and miracles a necessary accompaniment to the witness of the early church? Can you base your answer on a Biblical principle? Which of the following reflects best a possible reason for miracles in the Book of Acts:

to show God's power
to show man's power
to create interest in the message of the witness
as an "attention getter"

Was Peter's witness message planned? Does spontaneity mark most of the witness messages in the Book of Acts? Do you feel that Christians today tend to force the witness message? If so, how would you correct that tendency?

Christ's resurrection was the central theme of Peter's message. Find other passages in Acts and the rest of the New Testament that emphasize the resurrection. To begin, see I Corinthians 15:16-23. Use your concordance to determine the number of times the resurrection is referred to in the Book of Acts. How many times is it mentioned in connection with witnessing?

Do you think that Peter and John were the only believers witnessing in Jerusalem? Compare Peter's second witness message with his first. Then compare Peter's two messages with a typical witness message of today. Any similarities? Do we emphasize the death, burial, and especially the resurrection of Jesus?

## 5. WITNESSING DESPITE OPPOSITION (4:1-37)

AND as they spake unto the people, the priests, and the captain of the temple, and the Sadducees, came upon them,

2 Being grieved that they taught the people, and preached through Jesus the resurrection from the dead.

3 And they laid hands on them, and put *them* in hold unto the next day: for it was now eventide.

4 Howbeit many of them which heard the word believed; and the number of the men was about five thousand.

5 ¶ And it came to pass on the morrow, that their rulers, and elders, and scribes,

6 And Annas the high priest, and Cā̂i'-ă-phăs, and John, and Alexander, and as many as were of the kindred of the high priest, were gathered together at Jerusalem.

7 And when they had set them in the midst, they asked, By what power, or by what name, have ye done this?

8 Then Peter, filled with the Holy Ghost, said unto them, Ye rulers of the people, and elders of Israel,

9 If we this day be examined of the good deed done to the impotent man, by what means he is made whole;

10 Be it known unto you all, and to all the people of Israel, that by the name of Jesus Christ of Nazareth, whom ye crucified, whom God raised from the dead, *even* by him doth this man stand here before you whole.

11 This is the stone which was set at nought of you builders, which is become the head of the corner.

12 Neither is there salvation in any other: for there is none other name under heaven given among men, whereby we must be saved.

13 ¶ Now when they saw the boldness of Peter and John, and perceived that they were unlearned and ignorant men, they marvelled; and they took knowledge of them, that they had been with Jesus.

14 And beholding the man which was healed standing with them, they could say nothing against it.

15 But when they had commanded them to go aside out of the council, they conferred among themselves,

16 Saying, What shall we do to these men? for that indeed a notable miracle hath been done by them *is* manifest to all them that dwell in Jerusalem; and we cannot deny *it*.

17 But that it spread no further among the people, let us straitly threaten them, that they speak henceforth to no man in this name.

18 And they called them, and commanded them not to speak at all nor teach in the name of Jesus.

19 But Peter and John answered and said unto them, Whether it be right in the sight of God to hearken unto you more than unto God, judge ye.

20 For we cannot but speak the things which we have seen and heard.

21 So when they had further threatened them, they let them go, finding nothing how they might punish them, because of the people: for all *men* glorified God for that which was done.

22 For the man was above forty

years old, on whom this miracle of healing was shewed.

23 ¶ And being let go, they went to their own company, and reported all that the chief priests and elders had said unto them.

24 And when they heard that, they lifted up their voice to God with one accord, and said, Lord, thou *art* God, which hast made heaven, and earth, and the sea, and all that in them is:

25 Who by the mouth of thy servant David hast said, Why did the heathen rage, and the people imagine vain things?

26 The kings of the earth stood up, and the rulers were gathered together against the Lord, and against his Christ.

27 For of a truth against thy holy child Jesus, whom thou hast anointed, both Herod, and Pontius Pilate, with the Gentiles, and the people of Israel, were gathered together,

28 For to do whatsoever thy hand and thy counsel determined before to be done.

29 And now, Lord, behold their threatenings: and grant unto thy servants, that with all boldness they may speak thy word,

30 By stretching forth thine hand to heal; and that signs and wonders may be done by the name of thy holy child Jesus.

31 ¶ And when they had prayed, the place was shaken where they were assembled together; and they were all filled with the Holy Ghost, and they spake the word of God with boldness.

32 And the multitude of them that believed were of one heart and of one soul: neither said any *of them* that aught of the things which he possessed was his own; but they had all things common.

33 And with great power gave the apostles witness of the resurrection of the Lord Jesus: and great grace was upon them all.

34 Neither was there any among them that lacked: for as many as were possessors of lands or houses sold them, and brought the prices of the things that were sold,

35 And laid *them* down at the apostles' feet: and distribution was made unto every man according as he had need.

36 And Joses, who by the apostles was surnamed Barnabas, (which is, being interpreted, The son of consolation,) a Levite, *and* of the country of Cyprus,

37 Having land, sold *it*, and brought the money, and laid *it* at the apostles' feet.

List the hindrances to witnessing that you find in this passage. What group hindered the witnesses? Didn't everyone in that group believe in God? What was the difference between those who witnessed and those who tried to stop the witnesses? Point out the differences today between being religious and being a Christian.

Notice how Peter turned the delay and persecution into a witnessing opportunity. Illustrate from your own experience how a delay or hindrance gave you a chance to testify for Christ.

Can you find a better description or definition for witnessing than verse 20? Tie this in with verse 33.

It is obvious that Peter and John had no intention of obeying the command to stop speaking about Christ. How does this attitude square with Romans 13:1-7?

What effect did the threat from the religious authorities have on the witnesses? Based on verses 29 and 30, what was their attitude toward threats and persecution? Why is it that witnesses usually praise God no matter what the results?

So far, three witnessing experiences in Acts have been considered. Can you make a formula from them? Compare yours with this formula for witnessing:

a Spirit-filled witness
an "attention-getter" used
a question or desire to hear
a God-given opportunity
the gospel presented
a response

Now apply the formula to chapters three and four of Acts.

Was there a Spirit-filled witness? (4:8, 13, 33)
Was there an "attention-getter"? (3:6-11; 4:14)
Was there a question? (4:7)
Was there a God-given opportunity? (4:7a)
Was the gospel presented? (4:10-12)
What was the response? (4:17-18)

Keep this formula in the back of your mind as you study other witnessing experiences in Acts.

Relate one of your own witnessing opportunities. Was the "pattern" there? How was it similar? How was it different?

## 6. WITNESSING DESPITE TRIALS (5:1–6:7)

BUT a certain man named Ăn-ă-nī'-ăs, with Sapphira his wife, sold a possession,

2 And kept back *part* of the price, his wife also being privy *to it*, and brought a certain part, and laid *it* at the apostles' feet.

3 But Peter said, Ăn-ă-nī'-ăs, why hath Satan filled thine heart to lie to the Holy Ghost, and to keep back *part* of the price of the land?

4 Whiles it remained, was it not thine own? and after it was sold, was it not in thine own power? why hast thou conceived this thing in thine heart? thou hast not lied unto men, but unto God.

5 And Ăn-ă-nī'-ăs hearing these words fell down, and gave up the ghost: and great fear came on all them that heard these things.

6 And the young men arose, wound him up, and carried *him* out, and buried *him*.

7 And it was about the space of three hours after, when his wife, not knowing what was done, came in.

8 And Peter answered unto her, Tell me whether ye sold the land for so much? And she said, Yea, for so much.

9 Then Peter said unto her, How is it that ye have agreed together to tempt the Spirit of the Lord? behold, the feet of them which have buried thy husband *are* at the door, and shall carry thee out.

10 Then fell she down straightway at his feet, and yielded up the ghost: and the young men came in, and found her dead, and, carrying *her* forth, buried *her* by her husband.

11 And great fear came upon all the church, and upon as many as heard these things.

12 ¶ And by the hands of the apostles were many signs and wonders wrought among the people; (and they were all with one accord in Solomon's porch.

13 And of the rest durst no man join himself to them: but the people magnified them.

14 And believers were the more added to the Lord, multitudes both of men and women.)

15 Insomuch that they brought forth the sick into the streets, and laid *them* on beds and couches, that at the least the shadow of Peter passing by might overshadow some of them.

16 There came also a multitude *out* of the cities round about unto Jerusalem, bringing sick folks, and them which were vexed with

unclean spirits: and they were healed every one.

17 ¶ Then the high priest rose up, and all they that were with him, (which is the sect of the Sadducees,) and were filled with indignation,

18 And laid their hands on the apostles, and put them in the common prison.

19 But the angel of the Lord by night opened the prison doors, and brought them forth, and said,

20 Go, stand and speak in the temple to the people all the words of this life.

21 And when they heard *that*, they entered into the temple early in the morning, and taught. But the high priest came, and they that were with him, and called the council together, and all the senate of the children of Israel, and sent to the prison to have them brought.

22 But when the officers came, and found them not in the prison, they returned, and told,

23 Saying, The prison truly found we shut with all safety, and the keepers standing without before the doors: but when we had opened, we found no man within.

24 Now when the high priest and the captain of the temple and the chief priests heard these things, they doubted of them whereunto this would grow.

25 Then came one and told them, saying, Behold, the men whom ye put in prison are standing in the temple, and teaching the people.

26 Then went the captain with the officers, and brought them without violence: for they feared the people, lest they should have been stoned.

27 And when they had brought them, they set *them* before the council: and the high priest asked them,

28 Saying, Did not we straitly command you that ye should not teach in this name? and, behold, ye have filled Jerusalem with your doctrine, and intend to bring this man's blood upon us.

29 ¶ Then Peter and the *other* apostles answered and said, We ought to obey God rather than men.

30 The God of our fathers raised up Jesus, whom ye slew and hanged on a tree.

31 Him hath God exalted with his right hand *to be* a Prince and a Saviour, for to give repentance to Israel, and forgiveness of sins.

32 And we are his witnesses of these things; and *so is* also the Holy Ghost, whom God hath given to them that obey him.

33 ¶ When they heard *that*, they were cut *to the heart*, and took counsel to slay them.

34 Then stood there up one in the council, a Pharisee named Gă-mā′-lĭ-ĕl, a doctor of the law, had in reputation among all the people, and commanded to put the apostles forth a little space;

35 And said unto them, Ye men of Israel, take heed to yourselves what ye intend to do as touching these men.

36 For before these days rose up Thêu′-dăs, boasting himself to be somebody; to whom a number of men, about four hundred, joined themselves: who was slain; and all, as many as obeyed him, were scattered, and brought to nought.

37 After this man rose up Judas of Galilee in the days of the taxing, and drew away much people after him: he also perished; and all, *even* as many as obeyed him, were dispersed.

38 And now I say unto you, Refrain from these men, and let them alone: for if this counsel or this work be of men, it will come to nought:

39 But if it be of God, ye cannot overthrow it; lest haply ye be found even to fight against God.

40 And to him they agreed: and when they had called the apostles, and beaten *them*, they commanded that they should not speak in the name of Jesus, and let them go.

41 ¶ And they departed from the presence of the council, re-

joicing that they were counted worthy to suffer shame for his name.

42 And daily in the temple, and in every house, they ceased not to teach and preach Jesus Christ.

CHAPTER 6

AND in those days, when the number of the disciples was multiplied, there arose a murmuring of the Grecians against the Hebrews, because their widows were neglected in the daily ministration.

2 Then the twelve called the multitude of the disciples *unto them*, and said, It is not reason that we should leave the word of God, and serve tables.

3 Wherefore, brethren, look ye out among you seven men of honest report, full of the Holy Ghost and wisdom, whom we may appoint over this business.

4 But we will give ourselves continually to prayer, and to the ministry of the word.

5 ¶ And the saying pleased the whole multitude: and they chose Stephen, a man full of faith and of the Holy Ghost, and Philip, and Prŏch′-ŏ-rŭs, and Nī-cā′-nôr, and Timon, and Pär′-mĕ-năs, and Nicolas a proselyte of Ăn′-tĭ-ŏch:

6 Whom they set before the apostles: and when they had prayed, they laid *their* hands on them.

7 And the word of God increased; and the number of the disciples multiplied in Jerusalem greatly; and a great company of the priests were obedient to the faith.

In this passage the witnesses are confronted with three problems:

problems from fakes within (5:1-16)
problems from forces without (5:17-42)
problems from finances within (6:1-7)

Who were the fakes in 1-16; How were they a problem to the witnesses? Give another name for fake. Are fakes Christians? Can you prove from Acts 4:31–5:16 that Ananias and Sapphira probably were not even saved?

Are problems good or bad for the witnessing church? Does every problem have a solution? In this passage who was responsible for the problem? For the solution? What was the solution? Were the results favorable or unfavorable?

Are there false witnesses within the church today who

are not "of" the church? If so, how are they causing problems in relationship to witnessing?

As you read through the Book of Acts, notice the continual battle between God and Satan. Why would Satan desire to cause problems for the witnesses? Why should the witness be especially aware of Satan?

How can "religious" leaders be used by Satan to thwart witnessing (see 5:17-42)? Why didn't the apostles obey the threats of the religious leaders of their day?

How did Peter react to persecution? From this passage give specific instances of how Satan tried to hinder witnessing. How did God overrule?

Did Peter change his message when he witnessed to the religious hierarchy? What did he emphasize? Should a witness be the same for all people?

How did finances threaten to interfere with the witnessing work? What was God's solution? In what way did Satan's "dart" backfire?

Is the phrase, "the Word of God increased," synonymous with witnessing?

Did the deacons have a responsibility to witness? Prove your answer.

Does 6:5 tell us that not all first-century Christians were full of the Holy Spirit all the time? Could they have been effective witnesses without being "full of the Holy Spirit"?

# 7. WITNESSING UNTIL DEATH (6:8–7:60)

8 And Stephen, full of faith and power, did great wonders and miracles among the people.

9 ¶ Then there arose certain of the synagogue, which is called *the synagogue* of the Lī-bĕr′-tīnes, and Çȳ-rē′-nĭ-ăns, and Alexandrians, and of them of Çī-lĭç′-ĭ-ă and of Asia, disputing with Stephen.

10 And they were not able to resist the wisdom and the spirit by which he spake.

11 Then they suborned men, which said, We have heard him speak blasphemous words against Moses, and *against* God.

12 And they stirred up the people, and the elders, and the scribes, and came upon *him*, and caught him, and brought *him* to the council,

13 And set up false witnesses, which said, This man ceaseth not to speak blasphemous words against this holy place, and the law:

14 For we have heard him say, that this Jesus of Nazareth shall destroy this place, and shall change the customs which Moses delivered us.

15 And all that sat in the council, looking stedfastly on him, saw his face as it had been the face of an angel.

## CHAPTER 7

THEN said the high priest, Are these things so?

2 And he said, Men, brethren, and fathers, hearken; The God of glory appeared unto our father Abraham, when he was in Mĕs-ŏ-pŏ-tā′-mĭ-ă, before he dwelt in Chăr′-răn,

3 And said unto him, Get thee out of thy country, and from thy kindred, and come into the land which I shall shew thee.

4 Then came he out of the land of the Chăl-dæ′-ăns, and dwelt in Chăr′-răn: and from thence, when his father was dead, he removed him into this land, wherein ye now dwell.

5 And he gave him none inheritance in it, no, not *so much as* to set his foot on: yet he promised that he would give it to him for a possession, and to his seed after him, when *as yet* he had no child.

6 And God spake on this wise, That his seed should sojourn in a strange land; and that they should bring them into bondage, and entreat *them* evil four hundred years.

7 And the nation to whom they shall be in bondage will I judge, said God: and after that shall they come forth, and serve me in this place.

8 And he gave him the covenant of circumcision: and so *Abraham* begat Isaac, and circumcised him the eighth day; and Isaac *begat* Jacob; and Jacob *begat* the twelve patriarchs.

9 And the patriarchs, moved with envy, sold Joseph into Egypt: but God was with him,

10 And delivered him out of all his afflictions, and gave him favour and wisdom in the sight of Phâr′-ā̄ŏh king of Egypt; and he made him governor over Egypt and all his house.

11 Now there came a dearth over all the land of Egypt and Chā′-nă-ăn, and great affliction: and our fathers found no sustenance.

12 But when Jacob heard that there was corn in Egypt, he sent out our fathers first.

13 And at the second *time* Joseph was made known to his brethren; and Joseph's kindred was made known unto Phâr′-ā̄ŏh.

14 Then sent Joseph, and called his father Jacob to *him*, and all his kindred, threescore and fifteen souls.

15 So Jacob went down into Egypt, and died, he, and our fathers,

16 And were carried over into Sȳ′-chĕm, and laid in the sepulchre that Abraham bought for a sum of money of the sons of Ĕm′-môr *the father* of Sychem.

17 But when the time of the promise drew nigh, which God

had sworn to Abraham, the people grew and multiplied in Egypt,

18 Till another king arose, which knew not Joseph.

19 The same dealt subtilly with our kindred, and evil entreated our fathers, so that they cast out their young children, to the end they might not live.

20 In which time Moses was born, and was exceeding fair, and nourished up in his father's house three months:

21 And when he was cast out, Phâr′-ā̄ōh's daughter took him up, and nourished him for her own son.

22 And Moses was learned in all the wisdom of the Egyptians, and was mighty in words and in deeds.

23 And when he was full forty years old, it came into his heart to visit his brethren the children of Israel.

24 And seeing one *of them* suffer wrong, he defended *him*, and avenged him that was oppressed, and smote the Egyptian:

25 For he supposed his brethren would have understood how that God by his hand would deliver them: but they understood not.

26 And the next day he shewed himself unto them as they strove, and would have set them at one again, saying, Sirs, ye are brethren; why do ye wrong one to another?

27 But he that did his neighbour wrong thrust him away, saying, Who made thee a ruler and a judge over us?

28 Wilt thou kill me, as thou diddest the Egyptian yesterday?

29 Then fled Moses at this saying, and was a stranger in the land of Madian, where he begat two sons.

30 And when forty years were expired, there appeared to him in the wilderness of mount Sina an angel of the Lord in a flame of fire in a bush.

31 When Moses saw *it*, he wondered at the sight: and as he drew near to behold *it*, the voice of the Lord came unto him,

32 *Saying*, I *am* the God of thy fathers, the God of Abraham, and the God of Isaac, and the God of Jacob. Then Moses trembled, and durst not behold.

33 Then said the Lord to him, Put off thy shoes from thy feet: for the place where thou standest is holy ground.

34 I have seen, I have seen the affliction of my people which is in Egypt, and I have heard their groaning, and am come down to deliver them. And now come, I will send thee into Egypt.

35 This Moses whom they refused, saying, Who made thee a ruler and a judge? the same did God send *to be* a ruler and a deliverer by the hand of the angel which appeared to him in the bush.

36 He brought them out, after that he had shewed wonders and signs in the land of Egypt, and in the Red sea, and in the wilderness forty years.

37 ¶ This is that Moses, which said unto the children of Israel, A prophet shall the Lord your God raise up unto you of your brethren, like unto me; him shall ye hear.

38 This is he, that was in the church in the wilderness with the angel which spake to him in the mount Sina, and *with* our fathers: who received the lively oracles to give unto us:

39 To whom our fathers would not obey, but thrust *him* from them, and in their hearts turned back again into Egypt,

40 Saying unto Aaron, Make us gods to go before us: for *as for* this Moses, which brought us out of the land of Egypt, we wot not what is become of him.

41 And they made a calf in those days, and offered sacrifice unto the idol, and rejoiced in the works of their own hands.

42 Then God turned, and gave them up to worship the host of heaven; as it is written in the book of the prophets, O ye house of Israel, have ye offered to me slain beasts and sacrifices *by the space of* forty years in the wilderness?

43 Yea, ye took up the tabernacle of Mō′-lŏch, and the star of your god Remphan, figures which ye made to worship them: and I

will carry you away beyond Babylon.

44 Our fathers had the tabernacle of witness in the wilderness, as he had appointed, speaking unto Moses, that he should make it according to the fashion that he had seen.

45 Which also our fathers that came after brought in with Jesus into the possession of the Gentiles, whom God drave out before the face of our fathers, unto the days of David;

46 Who found favour before God, and desired to find a tabernacle for the God of Jacob.

47 But Solomon built him an house.

48 Howbeit the most High dwelleth not in temples made with hands; as saith the prophet,

49 Heaven *is* my throne, and earth *is* my footstool: what house will ye build me? saith the Lord: or what *is* the place of my rest?

50 Hath not my hand made all these things?

51 ¶ Ye stiffnecked and uncircumcised in heart and ears, ye do always resist the Holy Ghost: as your fathers *did*, so *do* ye.

52 Which of the prophets have not your fathers persecuted? and they have slain them which shewed before of the coming of the Just One; of whom ye have been now the betrayers and murderers:

53 Who have received the law by the disposition of angels, and have not kept *it*.

54 ¶ When they heard these things, they were cut to the heart, and they gnashed on him with *their* teeth.

55 But he, being full of the Holy Ghost, looked up stedfastly into heaven, and saw the glory of God, and Jesus standing on the right hand of God,

56 And said, Behold, I see the heavens opened, and the Son of man standing on the right hand of God.

57 Then they cried out with a loud voice, and stopped their ears, and ran upon him with one accord,

58 And cast *him* out of the city, and stoned *him:* and the witnesses laid down their clothes at a young man's feet, whose name was Saul.

59 And they stoned Stephen, calling upon *God*, and saying, Lord Jesus, receive my spirit.

60 And he kneeled down, and cried with a loud voice, Lord, lay not this sin to their charge. And when he had said this, he fell asleep.

Would Stephen have gotten into trouble if he'd just served tables? Does the fact that Stephen witnessed prove that witnessing was done by *all* first-century Christians? Name other witnesses in the Book of Acts besides the apostles.

Is it good for a witness to get into an argument as Stephen did (6:9)? Why were the "religious" leaders so incensed by Stephen's witness? Note the phrase "they were not able to resist the wisdom and spirit by which he spake."

Stephen was asked a simple question (7:1). Recall other questions that offered an opportunity to witness for Jesus Christ. Are questions from unbelievers important? Read I Peter 3:15 before giving your answer. As you work your way through the Book of Acts, watch for questions that lead to a witnessing opportunity.

How can we lead a person to ask a question that will develop into a witnessing opportunity? Why is it wise to wait for an unbeliever to ask a question? Relate a witnessing opportunity you had because of a question from a non-Christian.

In answer to a very short question, Stephen delivered a lengthy witness message. Is it the longest recorded in the Book of Acts? What should determine the length of a witness message?

What was the content of Stephen's message? Why, do you suppose, did he include so much history of Israel?

Notice how knowledgable Stephen was in the Scriptures. Why is knowledge of the Scriptures important for the witness? What knowledge is basic for a witness? Should lack of extensive Biblical knowledge cause one to avoid witnessing? What specific steps can a witness take to improve his knowledge of the Scriptures?

What was the result of Stephen's witnessing? Does that make Stephen a total failure as a witness? Why, or why not? Should a witness expect to win everyone he witnesses to? Is there a difference between soul winning and witnessing?

List the characteristics of Stephen that were Christ-like. Scan 7:8–7:60 for your answer. Why would all witnesses be more effective if they were more Christ-like? How can a witness develop Christ-like characteristics?

How does *Phase One:* In Jerusalem (Acts 2:1–7:60) lay the groundwork for *Phase Two:* In all Judaea and Samaria?

## *PHASE TWO: WITNESSING IN JUDAEA AND SAMARIA (8:1–12:25)*

# 8. SAMARIA RESPONDS TO A WITNESS (8:1-25)

## CHAPTER 8

AND Saul was consenting unto his death. And at that time there was a great persecution against the church which was at Jerusalem; and they were all scattered abroad throughout the regions of Judæa and Samaria, except the apostles.

2 And devout men carried Stephen *to his burial*, and made great lamentation over him.

3 As for Saul, he made havoc of the church, entering into every house, and haling men and women committed *them* to prison.

4 Therefore they that were scattered abroad went every where preaching the word.

5 Then Philip went down to the city of Samaria, and preached Christ unto them.

6 And the people with one accord gave heed unto those things which Philip spake, hearing and seeing the miracles which he did.

7 For unclean spirits, crying with loud voice, came out of many that were possessed *with them:* and many taken with palsies, and that were lame, were healed.

8 And there was great joy in that city.

9 But there was a certain man, called Simon, which beforetime in the same city used sorcery, and bewitched the people of Samaria, giving out that himself was some great one:

10 To whom they all gave heed, from the least to the greatest, saying, This man is the great power of God.

11 And to him they had regard, because that of long time he had bewitched them with sorceries.

12 But when they believed Philip preaching the things concerning the kingdom of God, and the name of Jesus Christ, they were baptized, both men and women.

13 Then Simon himself believed also: and when he was baptized, he continued with Philip, and wondered, beholding the miracles and signs which were done.

14 Now when the apostles which were at Jerusalem heard that Samaria had received the word of God, they sent unto them Peter and John:

15 Who, when they were come down, prayed for them, that they might receive the Holy Ghost:

16 (For as yet he was fallen upon none of them: only they were baptized in the name of the Lord Jesus.)

17 Then laid they *their* hands on them, and they received the Holy Ghost.

18 And when Simon saw that through laying on of the apostles' hands the Holy Ghost was given, he offered them money,

19 Saying, Give me also this power, that on whomsoever I lay hands, he may receive the Holy Ghost.

20 But Peter said unto him, Thy money perish with thee, because thou hast thought that the gift of God may be purchased with money.

21 Thou hast neither part nor lot in this matter: for thy heart is not right in the sight of God.

22 Repent therefore of this thy wickedness, and pray God, if perhaps the thought of thine heart may be forgiven thee.

23 For I perceive that thou art in the gall of bitterness, and *in* the bond of iniquity.

24 Then answered Simon, and said, Pray ye to the Lord for me, that none of these things which ye have spoken come upon me.

25 And they, when they had testified and preached the word of the Lord, returned to Jerusalem, and preached the gospel in many villages of the Samaritans.

Consult a Bible map of Palestine to determine the area covered by *Phase Two:* Judaea and Samaria.

Did Stephen's witness have any immediate effect on Saul [Paul]? Any long-range effect (22:20)?

What can you learn about witnessing from verse 4?

What part did persecution play in God's plan to spread the gospel?

Verse 5 says that "Philip went down to a city in Samaria and proclaimed Christ there." Is this the same as "preached the word" in verse 4? Are both synonymous with witnessing? Why, or why not? Compare verses 4 and 5 with verse 25.

How did Philip gain the attention of the Samaritans? What were the results of Philip's witness in Samaria?

Why didn't the apostles flee from Jerusalem? How does a witness know when to go and when to stay?

## 9. A EUNUCH RESPONDS TO A WITNESS (8:26-40)

26 And the angel of the Lord spake unto Philip, saying, Arise, and go toward the south unto the way that goeth down from Jerusalem unto Gaza, which is desert.

27 And he arose and went: and, behold, a man of Ethiopia, an eunuch of great authority under Căn'-dă-çē queen of the Ethiopians, who had the charge of all her treasure, and had come to Jerusalem for to worship,

28 Was returning, and sitting in his chariot read Ē-șâi'-ăs the prophet.

29 Then the Spirit said unto Philip, Go near, and join thyself to this chariot.

30 And Philip ran thither to *him*, and heard him read the prophet Ē-șâi'-ăs, and said, Understandest thou what thou readest?

31 And he said, How can I, except some man should guide me? And he desired Philip that he would come up and sit with him.

32 The place of the scripture which he read was this, He was led as a sheep to the slaughter; and like a lamb dumb before his shearer, so opened he not his mouth:

33 In his humiliation his judgment was taken away: and who shall declare his generation? for his life is taken from the earth.

34 And the eunuch answered Philip, and said, I pray thee, of whom speaketh the prophet this? of himself, or of some other man?

35 Then Philip opened his mouth, and began at the same scripture, and preached unto him Jesus.

36 And as they went on *their* way, they came unto a certain water: and the eunuch said, See, *here is* water; what doth hinder me to be baptized?

37 And Philip said, If thou believest with all thine heart, thou mayest. And he answered and said, I believe that Jesus Christ is the Son of God.

38 And he commanded the chariot to stand still: and they went down both into the water, both Philip and the eunuch; and he baptized him.

39 And when they were come up out of the water, the Spirit of the Lord caught away Philip, that the eunuch saw him no more: and he went on his way rejoicing.

40 But Philip was found at Ă-zō′-tŭs: and passing through he preached in all the cities, till he came to Cæsarea.

Acts records many witnessing experiences. How many? Notice the various aspects of witnessing found in this excellent example.

Compare this passage with God's pattern for witnessing:

Was Philip filled with the Holy Spirit?
Was Philip directed by the Lord?
What "attention-getter" was used?
What was the response of the eunuch to the "attention-getter"?
What was the result?

## 10. A PERSECUTOR RESPONDS TO A WITNESS (9:1-31)

CHAPTER 9

AND Saul, yet breathing out threatenings and slaughter against the disciples of the Lord, went unto the high priest,

2 And desired of him letters to Damascus to the synagogues, that if he found any of this way, whether they were men or women, he might bring them bound unto Jerusalem.

3 And as he journeyed, he came near Damascus: and suddenly there shined round about him a light from heaven:

4 And he fell to the earth, and heard a voice saying unto him, Saul, Saul, why persecutest thou me?

5 And he said, Who art thou, Lord? And the Lord said, I am Jesus whom thou persecutest: *it*

*is* hard for thee to kick against the pricks.

6 And he trembling and astonished said, Lord, what wilt thou have me to do? And the Lord *said* unto him, Arise, and go into the city, and it shall be told thee what thou must do.

7 And the men which journeyed with him stood speechless, hearing a voice, but seeing no man.

8 And Saul arose from the earth; and when his eyes were opened, he saw no man: but they led him by the hand, and brought *him* into Damascus.

9 And he was three days without sight, and neither did eat nor drink.

10 ¶ And there was a certain disciple at Damascus, named Ăn-ă-nī′-ăs; and to him said the Lord in a vision, Ananias. And he said, Behold, I *am here*, Lord.

11 And the Lord *said* unto him, Arise, and go into the street which is called Straight, and inquire in the house of Judas for *one* called Saul, of Tarsus: for, behold, he prayeth,

12 And hath seen in a vision a man named Ăn-ă-nī′-ăs coming in, and putting *his* hand on him, that he might receive his sight.

13 Then Ăn-ă-nī′-ăs answered, Lord, I have heard by many of this man, how much evil he hath done to thy saints at Jerusalem:

14 And here he hath authority from the chief priests to bind all that call on thy name.

15 But the Lord said unto him, Go thy way: for he is a chosen vessel unto me, to bear my name before the Gentiles, and kings, and the children of Israel:

16 For I will shew him how great things he must suffer for my name's sake.

17 And Ăn-ă-nī′-ăs went his way, and entered into the house; and putting his hands on him said, Brother Saul, the Lord, *even* Jesus, that appeared unto thee in the way as thou camest, hath sent me, that thou mightest receive thy sight, and be filled with the Holy Ghost.

18 And immediately there fell from his eyes as it had been scales: and he received sight forthwith, and arose, and was baptized.

19 And when he had received meat, he was strengthened. Then was Saul certain days with the disciples which were at Damascus.

20 And straightway he preached Christ in the synagogues, that he is the Son of God.

21 But all that heard *him* were amazed, and said; Is not this he that destroyed them which called on this name in Jerusalem, and came hither for that intent, that he might bring them bound unto the chief priests?

22 But Saul increased the more in strength, and confounded the Jews which dwelt at Damascus, proving that this is very Christ.

23 ¶ And after that many days were fulfilled, the Jews took counsel to kill him:

24 But their laying await was known of Saul. And they watched the gates day and night to kill him.

25 Then the disciples took him by night, and let *him* down by the wall in a basket.

26 And when Saul was come to Jerusalem, he assayed to join himself to the disciples: but they were all afraid of him, and believed not that he was a disciple.

27 But Barnabas took him, and brought *him* to the apostles, and declared unto them how he had seen the Lord in the way, and that he had spoken to him, and how he had preached boldly at Damascus in the name of Jesus.

28 And he was with them coming in and going out at Jerusalem.

29 And he spake boldly in the name of the Lord Jesus, and disputed against the Grecians: but they went about to slay him.

30 *Which* when the brethren knew, they brought him down to Cæsarea, and sent him forth to Tarsus.

31 Then had the churches rest throughout all Judæa and Galilee and Samaria, and were edified; and walking in the fear of the Lord, and in the comfort of the Holy Ghost, were multiplied.

God's witnessing program had three phases (1:8). What groundwork did God lay in the first two phases that prepared the witnesses for *Phase Three?*

List the characteristics Saul possessed prior to his conversion that would make him an unusually good witness for Christ? Who had witnessed to Saul before the events recorded in Chapter 9?

Saul describes his conversion in 26:13-18. List other references Paul makes to his conversion throughout Acts and in his epistles.

Witnesses are not always permitted to "follow through" and "win" a soul to Christ. Can witnessing be compared to "sowing the seed?" Refer to I Corinthians 3:6-9.

According to 26:13-18, what was Saul chosen to do? Compare 26:13-18 with 9:15-16. What definition for witnessing is found in 9:15? Why was Ananias sent to Saul? What did Saul do immediately after he was filled with the Holy Spirit?

How long should a convert wait before witnessing? What are the qualifications of a witness? Compare Paul's conversion with that of the Ethiopian eunuch. What can you learn from these two accounts?

So far witnessing for Christ both to groups (mass evangelism) and individually (one-to-one) has been discussed. Do both types of witnessing fit into God's program?

In verse 30 the brethren sent Saul back home to Tarsus. Why? Do you feel it is harder to witness to your own family or to total strangers? Why should one be more difficult than the other?

Some Christians have witnessed to their families and experienced a chain reaction. Have you had a reaction to your witness to an unsaved close friend or family member? Can you illustrate a chain reaction to witnessing from the Book of Acts?

## 11. JUDAEA RESPONDS TO A WITNESS (9:32-43)

32 ¶ And it came to pass, as Peter passed throughout all *quarters*, he came down also to the saints which dwelt at Lydda.

33 And there he found a certain man named Æ-nē′-ăs, which had kept his bed eight years, and was sick of the palsy.

34 And Peter said unto him, Æ-nē′-ăs, Jesus Christ maketh thee whole: arise, and make thy bed. And he arose immediately.

35 And all that dwelt at Lydda and Saron saw him, and turned to the Lord.

36 ¶ Now there was at Joppa a certain disciple named Tabitha, which by interpretation is called Dorcas: this woman was full of good works and almsdeeds which she did.

37 And it came to pass in those days, that she was sick, and died: whom when they had washed, they laid *her* in an upper chamber.

38 And forasmuch as Lydda was nigh to Joppa, and the disciples had heard that Peter was there, they sent unto him two men, desiring *him* that he would not delay to come to them.

39 Then Peter arose and went with them. When he was come, they brought him into the upper chamber: and all the widows stood by him weeping, and shewing the coats and garments which Dorcas made, while she was with them.

40 But Peter put them all forth, and kneeled down, and prayed; and turning *him* to the body said, Tabitha, arise. And she opened her eyes: and when she saw Peter, she sat up.

41 And he gave her *his* hand, and lifted her up, and when he had called the saints and widows, presented her alive.

42 And it was known throughout all Joppa; and many believed in the Lord.

43 And it came to pass, that he tarried many days in Joppa with one Simon a tanner.

In this passage Peter continues to witness and to perform mighty miracles. What was the result of Peter's witness in Lydda?

Peter's next mighty wonder was the raising of Dorcas, the worker of good deeds, from the dead. Some would call doing good works witnessing. Do you? Why, or why not? Must a witness always be verbal? Keep in mind the definition of witnessing.

Would you say that doing good deeds is an "attention-getter" that provides opportunities to witness? This passage doesn't say that Dorcas witnessed for Christ, but she is called a disciple. Can one be a disciple and not witness? Explain your answer. List specific ways that good works might open the door for witnessing.

Illustrate how something you did for someone else gave you an opportunity to witness.

## 12. A CENTURION RESPONDS TO A WITNESS (10:1–11:30)

CHAPTER 10

THERE was a certain man in Cæsarea called Cornelius, a centurion of the band called the Italian *band*,

2 A devout *man*, and one that feared God with all his house, which gave much alms to the people, and prayed to God alway.

3 He saw in a vision evidently about the ninth hour of the day an angel of God coming in to him, and saying unto him, Cornelius.

4 And when he looked on him, he was afraid, and said, What is it, Lord? And he said unto him, Thy prayers and thine alms are come up for a memorial before God.

5 And now send men to Joppa, and call for *one* Simon, whose surname is Peter:

6 He lodgeth with one Simon a tanner, whose house is by the sea side: he shall tell thee what thou oughtest to do.

7 And when the angel which spake unto Cornelius was departed, he called two of his household servants, and a devout soldier of them that waited on him continually;

8 And when he had declared all *these* things unto them, he sent them to Joppa.

9 ¶ On the morrow, as they went on their journey, and drew nigh unto the city, Peter went up upon the housetop to pray about the sixth hour:

10 And he became very hungry, and would have eaten: but while they made ready, he fell into a trance,

11 And saw heaven opened, and a certain vessel descending unto him, as it had been a great sheet knit at the four corners, and let down to the earth:

12 Wherein were all manner of fourfooted beasts of the earth, and wild beasts, and creeping things, and fowls of the air.

13 And there came a voice to him, Rise, Peter; kill, and eat.

14 But Peter said, Not so, Lord; for I have never eaten any thing that is common or unclean.

15 And the voice *spake* unto him again the second time, What God hath cleansed, *that* call not thou common.

16 This was done thrice: and the vessel was received up again into heaven.

17 Now while Peter doubted in himself what this vision which he had seen should mean, behold, the men which were sent from Cornelius had made inquiry for Simon's house, and stood before the gate,

18 And called, and asked whether Simon, which was surnamed Peter, were lodged there.

19 ¶ While Peter thought on the vision, the Spirit said unto him, Behold, three men seek thee.

20 Arise therefore, and get thee down, and go with them, doubting nothing: for I have sent them.

21 Then Peter went down to the men which were sent unto him from Cornelius; and said, Behold, I am he whom ye seek: what *is* the cause wherefore ye are come?

22 And they said, Cornelius the centurion, a just man, and one that feareth God, and of good report among all the nation of the Jews, was warned from God by an holy angel to send for thee into his house, and to hear words of thee.

23 Then called he them in, and lodged *them*. And on the morrow Peter went away with them, and certain brethren from Joppa accompanied him.

24 And the morrow after they entered into Cæsarea. And Cornelius waited for them, and had called together his kinsmen and near friends.

25 And as Peter was coming in, Cornelius met him, and fell down at his feet, and worshipped *him*.

26 But Peter took him up, saying, Stand up; I myself also am a man.

27 And as he talked with him, he went in, and found many that were come together.

28 And he said unto them, Ye know how that it is an unlawful thing for a man that is a Jew to keep company, or come unto one of another nation; but God hath shewed me that I should not call any man common or unclean.

29 Therefore came I *unto you* without gainsaying, as soon as I was sent for: I ask therefore for what intent ye have sent for me?

30 And Cornelius said, Four days ago I was fasting until this hour; and at the ninth hour I prayed in my house, and, behold, a man stood before me in bright clothing,

31 And said, Cornelius, thy prayer is heard, and thine alms are had in remembrance in the sight of God.

32 Send therefore to Joppa, and call hither Simon, whose surname is Peter; he is lodged in the house of *one* Simon a tanner by the sea side: who, when he cometh, shall speak unto thee.

33 Immediately therefore I sent to thee; and thou hast well done that thou art come. Now therefore are we all here present before God, to hear all things that are commanded thee of God.

34 ¶ Then Peter opened *his* mouth, and said, Of a truth I perceive that God is no respecter of persons:

35 But in every nation he that feareth him, and worketh righteousness, is accepted with him.

36 The word which *God* sent unto the children of Israel, preaching peace by Jesus Christ: (he is Lord of all:)

37 That word, *I say*, ye know, which was published throughout all Judæa, and began from Galilee, after the baptism which John preached;

38 How God anointed Jesus of Nazareth with the Holy Ghost and with power: who went about doing good, and healing all that were oppressed of the devil; for God was with him.

39 And we are witnesses of all things which he did both in the land of the Jews, and in Jerusalem; whom they slew and hanged on a tree:

40 Him God raised up the third day, and shewed him openly;

41 Not to all the people, but unto witnesses chosen before of God, *even* to us, who did eat and drink with him after he rose from the dead.

42 And he commanded us to preach unto the people, and to testify that it is he which was ordained of God *to be* the Judge of quick and dead.

43 To him give all the prophets witness, that through his name whosoever believeth in him shall receive remission of sins.

44 ¶ While Peter yet spake these words, the Holy Ghost fell on all them which heard the word.

45 And they of the circumcision which believed were astonished, as many as came with Peter, because that on the Gentiles also was poured out the gift of the Holy Ghost.

46 For they heard them speak with tongues, and magnify God. Then answered Peter,

47 Can any man forbid water, that these should not be baptized, which have received the Holy Ghost as well as we?

48 And he commanded them to be baptized in the name of the Lord. Then prayed they him to tarry certain days.

## CHAPTER 11

AND the apostles and brethren that were in Judæa heard that the Gentiles had also received the word of God.

2 And when Peter was come up to Jerusalem, they that were of the circumcision contended with him,

3 Saying, Thou wentest in to men uncircumcised, and didst eat with them.

4 But Peter rehearsed *the matter* from the beginning, and expounded *it* by order unto them, saying,

5 I was in the city of Joppa praying: and in a trance I saw a vision, A certain vessel descend, as it had been a great sheet, let down from heaven by four corners; and it came even to me:

6 Upon the which when I had fastened mine eyes, I considered, and saw fourfooted beasts of the earth, and wild beasts, and creeping things, and fowls of the air.

7 And I heard a voice saying unto me, Arise, Peter; slay and eat.

8 But I said, Not so, Lord: for nothing common or unclean hath at any time entered into my mouth.

9 But the voice answered me again from heaven, What God hath cleansed, *that* call not thou common.

10 And this was done three times: and all were drawn up again into heaven.

11 And, behold, immediately there were three men already come unto the house where I was, sent from Cæsarea unto me.

12 And the Spirit bade me go with them, nothing doubting. Moreover these six brethren accompanied me, and we entered into the man's house:

13 And he shewed us how he had seen an angel in his house, which stood and said unto him, Send men to Joppa, and call for Simon, whose surname is Peter;

14 Who shall tell thee words, whereby thou and all thy house shall be saved.

15 And as I began to speak, the Holy Ghost fell on them, as on us at the beginning.

16 Then remembered I the word of the Lord, how that he said, John indeed baptized with water; but ye shall be baptized with the Holy Ghost.

17 Forasmuch then as God gave them the like gift as *he did* unto us, who believed on the Lord Jesus Christ; what was I, that I could withstand God?

18 When they heard these things, they held their peace, and glorified God, saying, Then hath God also to the Gentiles granted repentance unto life.

19 ¶ Now they which were scattered abroad upon the persecution that arose about Stephen travelled as far as Phē-nī′-çē, and Cyprus, and Ăn′-tĭ-ŏch, preaching the word to none but unto the Jews only.

20 And some of them were men of Cyprus and Çȳ-rē'-nē, which, when they were come to Ăn'-tĭ-ŏch, spake unto the Grecians, preaching the Lord Jesus.
21 And the hand of the Lord was with them: and a great number believed, and turned unto the Lord.
22 ¶ Then tidings of these things came unto the ears of the church which was in Jerusalem: and they sent forth Barnabas, that he should go as far as Ăn'-tĭ-ŏch.
23 Who, when he came, and had seen the grace of God, was glad, and exhorted them all, that with purpose of heart they would cleave unto the Lord.
24 For he was a good man, and full of the Holy Ghost and of faith: and much people was added unto the Lord.
25 Then departed Barnabas to Tarsus, for to seek Saul:
26 And when he had found him, he brought him unto Ăn'-tĭ-ŏch. And it came to pass, that a whole year they assembled themselves with the church, and taught much people. And the disciples were called Christians first in Antioch.
27 ¶ And in these days came prophets from Jerusalem unto Ăn'-tĭ-ŏch.
28 And there stood up one of them named Ăg'-ă-bŭs, and signified by the Spirit that there should be great dearth throughout all the world: which came to pass in the days of Claudius Cæsar.
29 Then the disciples, every man according to his ability, determined to send relief unto the brethren which dwelt in Judæa:
30 Which also they did, and sent it to the elders by the hands of Barnabas and Saul.

This section of Scripture can be divided into three divisions:

Peter, a prejudiced witness 10:1-18
Peter, a witness who loses his prejudice 10:19-48
Peter helps other witnesses to lose their prejudice 11:1-30

The fact that Peter stayed in Joppa several days with Simon the tanner is an indication that Peter's prejudices were beginning to soften. How does prejudice interfere with witnessing? List different kinds of prejudices. Why were the Jews prejudiced against the Gentiles? How deep-seated was this prejudice? Give illustrations.

How did God deal with Peter's prejudice? List other Bible passages that show that prejudices should not exist in the life of a Christian.

Give several examples from 10:19-48 which prove that Peter learned his lesson well. Why was it important that Peter prove to Cornelius that he was not prejudiced? How did Peter do this?

Notice the question that preceded the witness of Peter (v. 29).

How did Peter's witness message to these Gentiles differ from the one given to the Jews (chap. 4)?

What other words for witness are found in verses 22, 37, 42? An enriching word study is reading through the Book of Acts, and listing all the words used to describe witnessing.

In verses 39-43 Peter talks about witnessing. What point does he emphasize?

Note the Gentiles' reaction to Peter's message. Notice how God worked step by step to reduce and eliminate Peter's prejudice against the Gentiles.

Was the problem of prejudice limited only to Peter? How widespread was it? How could it have hindered the future witness of the church? How was the problem resolved?

How did Peter convince the church leaders that witnessing to and fellowshiping with Gentiles was God's will?

List specific prejudices common today. How do these prejudices interfere with a Christian's witness? What steps would you suggest for eliminating prejudice in your own life? How do you cope with prejudice when you see it in another person?

Notice an effect of Stephen's martyrdom in verses 19-21.

Barnabas comes to the forefront. What made him a well-qualified witness? Do Christians need special gifts to witness, or are all Christians automatically qualified to witness? Give reasons for your answer.

## 13. HEROD RESPONDS TO THE WITNESSES (12:1-25)

CHAPTER 12

NOW about that time Herod the king stretched forth *his* hands to vex certain of the church.

2 And he killed James the brother of John with the sword.

3 And because he saw it pleased the Jews, he proceeded further to take Peter also. (Then were the days of unleavened bread.)

4 And when he had apprehended him, he put *him* in prison, and delivered *him* to four quaternions of soldiers to keep him; intending after Easter to bring him forth to the people.

5 Peter therefore was kept in prison: but prayer was made without ceasing of the church unto God for him.

6 And when Herod would have brought him forth, the same night Peter was sleeping between two soldiers, bound with two chains: and the keepers before the door kept the prison.

7 And, behold, the angel of the Lord came upon *him*, and a light shined in the prison: and he smote Peter on the side, and raised him up, saying, Arise up quickly. And his chains fell off from *his* hands.

8 And the angel said unto him, Gird thyself, and bind on thy sandals. And so he did. And he saith unto him, Cast thy garment about thee, and follow me.

9 And he went out, and followed him; and wist not that it was true which was done by the angel; but thought he saw a vision.

10 When they were past the first and the second ward, they came unto the iron gate that leadeth unto the city; which opened to them of his own accord: and they went out, and passed on through one street; and forthwith the angel departed from him.

11 And when Peter was come to himself, he said, Now I know of a surety, that the Lord hath sent his angel, and hath delivered me out of the hand of Herod, and *from* all the expectation of the people of the Jews.

12 And when he had considered *the thing*, he came to the house of Mary the mother of John, whose surname was Mark; where many were gathered together praying.

13 And as Peter knocked at the door of the gate, a damsel came to hearken, named Rhoda.

14 And when she knew Peter's voice, she opened not the gate for gladness, but ran in, and told how Peter stood before the gate.

15 And they said unto her, Thou art mad. But she constantly affirmed that it was even so. Then said they, It is his angel.

16 But Peter continued knocking: and when they had opened *the door*, and saw him, they were astonished.

17 But he, beckoning unto them with the hand to hold their peace, declared unto them how the Lord had brought him out of the prison. And he said, Go shew these things unto James, and to the brethren. And he departed, and went into another place.

18 Now as soon as it was day, there was no small stir among the soldiers, what was become of Peter.

19 And when Herod had sought for him, and found him not, he examined the keepers, and commanded that *they* should be put to death. And he went down from Judæa to Cæsarea, and *there* abode.

20 ¶ And Herod was highly displeased with them of Tyre and Sidon: but they came with one accord to him, and, having made Blastus the king's chamberlain their friend, desired peace; because their country was nourished by the king's *country*.

21 And upon a set day Herod, arrayed in royal apparel, sat upon his throne, and made an oration unto them.

22 And the people gave a shout, *saying, It is* the voice of a god, and not of a man.

23 And immediately the angel of the Lord smote him, because he gave not God the glory: and he was eaten of worms, and gave up the ghost.

24 ¶ But the word of God grew and multiplied.

25 And Barnabas and Saul returned from Jerusalem, when they had fulfilled *their* ministry, and took with them John, whose surname was Mark.

Persecution flared up again, but again it was a blessing instead of a hindrance. Why? Why didn't persecution stop the witnesses? How are witnesses persecuted today?

What profound effect did this experience have on Peter's life? What did he learn from this experience (v. 11)? Why were those who were praying for Peter surprised at his appearance? What were they asking for in Peter's behalf? Why is there a need for us to pray for our fellow witnesses? Specifically, what should we pray for in their behalf?

How was Satan's attack on the witnesses through Herod overruled by God? What is meant by the expression, "the word of God continued to increase and spread"? How is this accomplished? Find similar phrases in the Book of Acts.

Is it easier to witness during times of persecution and suffering? Why, or why not?

# *PHASE THREE: WITNESSING IN THE GENTILE WORLD (13:1–28:31)*

## 14. WITNESSING IN CYPRUS (13:1-12)

CHAPTER 13

NOW there were in the church that was at Ăn′-tĭ-ŏch certain prophets and teachers; as Barnabas, and Simeon that was called Niger, and Lucius of Çȳ-rē′-nē, and Măn′-ā-ĕn, which had been brought up with Herod the tē′-trärch, and Saul.

2 As they ministered to the Lord, and fasted, the Holy Ghost said, Separate me Barnabas and Saul for the work whereunto I have called them.

3 And when they had fasted and prayed, and laid *their* hands on them, they sent *them* away.

4 ¶ So they, being sent forth by the Holy Ghost, departed unto Sĕ-lēū′-çĭ-ă; and from thence they sailed to Cyprus.

5 And when they were at Săl′-ă-mĭs, they preached the word of God in the synagogues of the Jews: and they had also John to *their* minister.

6 And when they had gone through the isle unto Pā′-phŏs, they found a certain sorcerer, a false prophet, a Jew, whose name *was* Bar-jesus:

7 Which was with the deputy of the country, Sergius Paulus, a prudent man; who called for Barnabas and Saul, and desired to hear the word of God.

8 But Ĕl′-ȳ-măs the sorcerer (for so is his name by interpretation) withstood them, seeking to turn away the deputy from the faith.

9 Then Saul, (who also *is called* Paul,) filled with the Holy Ghost, set his eyes on him,

10 And said, O full of all subtilty and all mischief, *thou* child of the devil, *thou* enemy of all righteousness, wilt thou not cease to pervert the right ways of the Lord?

11 And now, behold, the hand of the Lord *is* upon thee, and thou shalt be blind, not seeing the sun for a season. And immediately there fell on him a mist and a darkness; and he went about seeking some to lead him by the hand.

12 Then the deputy, when he saw what was done, believed, being astonished at the doctrine of the Lord.

*Phase Three* of God's witnessing program is ready to begin. It was introduced in 12:24: "But the word of God grew and multiplied." Has the Word of God ever stopped increasing and spreading? How would you evaluate the results of witnessing today?

What do you think was the central reason for the growth of the Word (cf. vv. 2-9)?

Who sent out the witnesses? Why? Where were the witnesses sent? Prove that the Holy Spirit was already preparing hearts to receive the gospel (v. 7). Describe the encounter with Elymas.

What made Paul a successful witness in spite of opposition?

What was the "doctrine of the Lord" that Paul preached?

If witnesses are led by the Holy Spirit, can they trust the Holy Spirit to open every witness experience? How does a witness know when he is being led by the Holy Spirit to witness?

What clues as to a believer's part in witnessing can you find in this passage?

Do you agree with this statement: "Witnessing should be a Spirit-led, spontaneous expression of the truth about Christ." How would you define witnessing?

## 15. WITNESSING IN ASIA MINOR (13:13–14:28)

13 Now when Paul and his company loosed from Pā'-phŏs, they came to Perga in Pamphylia: and John departing from them returned to Jerusalem.

14 ¶ But when they departed from Perga, they came to Ăn'-tĭ-ŏch in Pĭ-sĭd'-ĭ-ă, and went into the synagogue on the sabbath day, and sat down.

15 And after the reading of the law and the prophets the rulers of the synagogue sent unto them, saying, *Ye* men *and* brethren, if ye have any word of exhortation for the people, say on.

16 Then Paul stood up, and beckoning with *his* hand said, Men of Israel, and ye that fear God, give audience.

17 The God of this people of Israel chose our fathers, and exalted the people when they dwelt as strangers in the land of Egypt, and with an high arm brought he them out of it.

18 And about the time of forty years suffered he their manners in the wilderness.

19 And when he had destroyed seven nations in the land of Chā'-nă-ăn, he divided their land to them by lot.

20 And after that he gave *unto*

*them* judges about the space of four hundred and fifty years, until Samuel the prophet.

21 And afterward they desired a king: and God gave unto them Saul the son of Cis, a man of the tribe of Benjamin, by the space of forty years.

22 And when he had removed him, he raised up unto them David to be their king; to whom also he gave testimony, and said, I have found David the *son* of Jesse, a man after mine own heart, which shall fulfil all my will.

23 Of this man's seed hath God according to *his* promise raised unto Israel a Saviour, Jesus:

24 When John had first preached before his coming the baptism of repentance to all the people of Israel.

25 And as John fulfilled his course, he said, Whom think ye that I am? I am not *he*. But, behold, there cometh one after me, whose shoes of *his* feet I am not worthy to loose.

26 Men *and* brethren, children of the stock of Abraham, and whosoever among you feareth God, to you is the word of this salvation sent.

27 For they that dwell at Jerusalem, and their rulers, because they knew him not, nor yet the voices of the prophets which are read every sabbath day, they have fulfilled *them* in condemning *him*.

28 And though they found no cause of death *in him*, yet desired they Pilate that he should be slain.

29 And when they had fulfilled all that was written of him, they took *him* down from the tree, and laid *him* in a sepulchre.

30 But God raised him from the dead:

31 And he was seen many days of them which came up with him from Galilee to Jerusalem, who are his witnesses unto the people.

32 And we declare unto you glad tidings, how that the promise which was made unto the fathers,

33 God hath fulfilled the same unto us their children, in that he hath raised up Jesus again; as it is also written in the second psalm, Thou art my Son, this day have I begotten thee.

34 And as concerning that he raised him up from the dead, *now* no more to return to corruption, he said on this wise, I will give you the sure mercies of David.

35 Wherefore he saith also in another *psalm*, Thou shalt not suffer thine Holy One to see corruption.

36 For David, after he had served his own generation by the will of God, fell on sleep, and was laid unto his fathers, and saw corruption:

37 But he, whom God raised again, saw no corruption.

38 ¶ Be it known unto you therefore, men *and* brethren, that through this man is preached unto you the forgiveness of sins:

39 And by him all that believe are justified from all things, from which ye could not be justified by the law of Moses.

40 Beware therefore, lest that come upon you, which is spoken of in the prophets;

41 Behold, ye despisers, and wonder, and perish: for I work a work in your days, a work which ye shall in no wise believe, though a man declare it unto you.

42 And when the Jews were gone out of the synagogue, the Gentiles besought that these words might be preached to them the next sabbath.

43 Now when the congregation was broken up, many of the Jews and religious proselytes followed Paul and Barnabas: who, speaking to them, persuaded them to continue in the grace of God.

44 ¶ And the next sabbath day came almost the whole city together to hear the word of God.

45 But when the Jews saw the multitudes, they were filled with envy, and spake against those things which were spoken by Paul, contradicting and blaspheming.

46 Then Paul and Barnabas waxed bold, and said, It was necessary that the word of God

should first have been spoken to you: but seeing ye put it from you, and judge yourselves unworthy of everlasting life, lo, we turn to the Gentiles.

47 For so hath the Lord commanded us, *saying*, I have set thee to be a light of the Gentiles, that thou shouldest be for salvation unto the ends of the earth.

48 And when the Gentiles heard this, they were glad, and glorified the word of the Lord: and as many as were ordained to eternal life believed.

49 And the word of the Lord was published throughout all the region.

50 But the Jews stirred up the devout and honourable women, and the chief men of the city, and raised persecution against Paul and Barnabas, and expelled them out of their coasts.

51 But they shook off the dust of their feet against them, and came unto Ī-cō′-nĭ-ŭm.

52 And the disciples were filled with joy, and with the Holy Ghost.

## CHAPTER 14

AND it came to pass in Ī-cō′-nĭ-ŭm, that they went both together into the synagogue of the Jews, and so spake, that a great multitude both of the Jews and also of the Greeks believed.

2 But the unbelieving Jews stirred up the Gentiles, and made their minds evil affected against the brethren.

3 Long time therefore abode they speaking boldly in the Lord, which gave testimony unto the word of his grace, and granted signs and wonders to be done by their hands.

4 But the multitude of the city was divided: and part held with the Jews, and part with the apostles.

5 And when there was an assault made both of the Gentiles, and also of the Jews with their rulers, to use *them* despitefully, and to stone them,

6 They were ware of *it*, and fled unto Lystra and Dĕr′-bē, cities of Lȳ-că-ō′-nĭ-ă, and unto the region that lieth round about:

7 And there they preached the gospel.

8 ¶ And there sat a certain man at Lystra, impotent in his feet, being a cripple from his mother's womb, who never had walked:

9 The same heard Paul speak: who stedfastly beholding him, and perceiving that he had faith to be healed,

10 Said with a loud voice, Stand upright on thy feet. And he leaped and walked.

11 And when the people saw what Paul had done, they lifted up their voices, saying in the speech of Lȳ-că-ō′-nĭ-ă, The gods are come down to us in the likeness of men.

12 And they called Barnabas, Jupiter; and Paul, Mĕr-cū′-rĭ-ŭs, because he was the chief speaker.

13 Then the priest of Jupiter, which was before their city, brought oxen and garlands unto the gates, and would have done sacrifice with the people.

14 *Which* when the apostles, Barnabas and Paul, heard *of*, they rent their clothes, and ran in among the people, crying out,

15 And saying, Sirs, why do ye these things? We also are men of like passions with you, and preach unto you that ye should turn from these vanities unto the living God, which made heaven, and earth, and the sea, and all things that are therein:

16 Who in times past suffered all nations to walk in their own ways.

17 Nevertheless he left not himself without witness, in that he did good, and gave us rain from heaven, and fruitful seasons, filling our hearts with food and gladness.

18 And with these sayings scarce restrained they the people, that they had not done sacrifice unto them.

19 ¶ And there came thither *certain* Jews from Ăn′-tĭ-ŏch and Ī-cō′-nĭ-ŭm, who persuaded the people, and, having stoned Paul, drew *him* out of the city, supposing he had been dead.

20 Howbeit, as the disciples stood round about him, he rose

up, and came into the city: and the next day he departed with Barnabas to Dĕr′-bē.

21 And when they had preached the gospel to that city, and had taught many, they returned again to Lystra, and *to* Ī-cō′-nĭ-ŭm, and Ăn′-tĭ-ŏch,

22 Confirming the souls of the disciples, *and* exhorting them to continue in the faith, and that we must through much tribulation enter into the kingdom of God.

23 And when they had ordained them elders in every church, and had prayed with fasting, they commended them to the Lord, on whom they believed.

24 And after they had passed throughout Pī-sĭd′-ĭ-ă, they came to Pamphylia.

25 And when they had preached the word in Perga, they went down into Ăt-tā′-lĭ-ă:

26 And thence sailed to Ăn′-tĭ-ŏch, from whence they had been recommended to the grace of God for the work which they fulfilled.

27 And when they were come, and had gathered the church together, they rehearsed all that God had done with them, and how he had opened the door of faith unto the Gentiles.

28 And there they abode long time with the disciples.

Why, do you suppose, did John return to Jerusalem (v. 13)? Does this mean he wasn't a witness any more? Is he ever heard of again in Acts? In the letters of Paul to the churches?

Notice that Paul and Barnabas seem to use the synagogue as the center for their witness. Was this an advantage?

Which verses contain Paul's witness message? Was his message different from the one he preached to the Jews in Jerusalem? Why, do you suppose, does he include so much Jewish history? What can today's witness learn from an outline of Paul's message?

Does the pattern for witnessing fit this message? Was there an "attention-getter"? What was it? Did it open an opportunity to witness? Was the gospel given? Which verses? What were the results?

In the light of 13:48b, why bother with witnessing?

Who spread the Word of the Lord throughout the whole region? Would Paul and Barnabas have had the time to do this?

Paul and Barnabas were "expelled" (a nice way to say thrown out). What was their reaction (v. 52)?

What results did the witnesses have in Iconium? How did Satan try to squelch their success there? According to 14:3, who was responsible for their success? To what extent: very little? little? much? entire?

Why were "signs and wonders" important for witnessing? Give an illustration from this passage. Would witnessing today be easier if it was accompanied by signs and wonders? From this passage tell how a witness should react to success, to opposition.

Would you say that the witnesses were wasting precious time by returning to places where they had previously witnessed? Why, or why not?

## 16. WITNESSING TO THE JERUSALEM COUNCIL (15:1-35)

CHAPTER 15

AND certain men which came down from Judæa taught the brethren, *and said*, Except ye be circumcised after the manner of Moses, ye cannot be saved.

2 When therefore Paul and Barnabas had no small dissension and disputation with them, they determined that Paul and Barnabas, and certain other of them, should go up to Jerusalem unto the apostles and elders about this question.

3 And being brought on their way by the church, they passed through Phē-nī'-çē and Samaria, declaring the conversion of the Gentiles: and they caused great joy unto all the brethren.

4 And when they were come to Jerusalem, they were received of the church, and *of* the apostles and elders, and they declared all

things that God had done with them.

5 But there rose up certain of the sect of the Pharisees which believed, saying, That it was needful to circumcise them, and to command *them* to keep the law of Moses.

6 ¶ And the apostles and elders came together for to consider of this matter.

7 And when there had been much disputing, Peter rose up, and said unto them, Men *and* brethren, ye know how that a good while ago God made choice among us, that the Gentiles by my mouth should hear the word of the gospel, and believe.

8 And God, which knoweth the hearts, bare them witness, giving them the Holy Ghost, even as *he did* unto us;

9 And put no difference between us and them, purifying their hearts by faith.

10 Now therefore why tempt ye God, to put a yoke upon the neck of the disciples, which neither our fathers nor we were able to bear?

11 But we believe that through the grace of the Lord Jesus Christ we shall be saved, even as they.

12 ¶ Then all the multitude kept silence, and gave audience to Barnabas and Paul, declaring what miracles and wonders God had wrought among the Gentiles by them.

13 ¶ And after they had held their peace, James answered, saying, Men *and* brethren, hearken unto me:

14 Simeon hath declared how God at the first did visit the Gentiles, to take out of them a people for his name.

15 And to this agree the words of the prophets; as it is written,

16 After this I will return, and will build again the tabernacle of David, which is fallen down; and I will build again the ruins thereof, and I will set it up:

17 That the residue of men might seek after the Lord, and all the Gentiles, upon whom my name is called, saith the Lord, who doeth all these things.

18 Known unto God are all his works from the beginning of the world.

19 Wherefore my sentence is, that we trouble not them, which from among the Gentiles are turned to God:

20 But that we write unto them, that they abstain from pollutions of idols, and *from* fornication, and *from* things strangled, and *from* blood.

21 For Moses of old time hath in every city them that preach him, being read in the synagogues every sabbath day.

22 Then pleased it the apostles and elders, with the whole church, to send chosen men of their own company to Ăn′-tĭ-ŏch with Paul and Barnabas; *namely*, Judas surnamed Barsabas, and Silas, chief men among the brethren:

23 And they wrote *letters* by them after this manner; The apostles and elders and brethren *send* greeting unto the brethren which are of the Gentiles in Ăn′-tĭ-ŏch and Syria and Çi-lĭç′-ĭ′-ă:

24 Forasmuch as we have heard, that certain which went out from us have troubled you with words, subverting your souls, saying, *Ye must* be circumcised, and keep the law: to whom we gave no *such* commandment:

25 It seemed good unto us, being assembled with one accord, to send chosen men unto you with our beloved Barnabas and Paul,

26 Men that have hazarded their lives for the name of our Lord Jesus Christ.

27 We have sent therefore Judas and Silas, who shall also tell *you* the same things by mouth.

28 For it seemed good to the Holy Ghost, and to us, to lay upon you no greater burden than these necessary things;

29 That ye abstain from meats offered to idols, and from blood, and from things strangled, and from fornication: from which if ye keep yourselves, ye shall do well. Fare ye well.

30 So when they were dismissed, they came to Ăn′-tĭ-ŏch: and when they had gathered the mul-

titude together, they delivered the epistle:

31 *Which* when they had read, they rejoiced for the consolation.

32 And Judas and Silas, being prophets also themselves, exhorted the brethren with many words, and confirmed *them*.

33 And after they had tarried *there* a space, they were let go in peace from the brethren unto the apostles.

34 Notwithstanding it pleased Silas to abide there still.

35 Paul also and Barnabas continued in Ăn′-tĭ-ŏch, teaching and preaching the word of the Lord, with many others also.

15:4b says . . . "they declared all things that God had done with them." Is this witnessing? Is there a witness by believers? How is it different from a witness to a non-Christian?

What false doctrine was taught in the churches (v. 1, 5)? How much emphasis should be placed today on forms, customs, practices, doctrinal differences? To what extent should a witness be concerned with doctrine?

To what extent is a witness responsible for instructing a convert? Is it necessary that a convert believe all the doctrines of the church he joins? Must he follow all the practices of a particular congregation? If not, why not? Which doctrines and practices are not essential for a person's salvation?

Did Peter believe that neither the Jew nor the Gentile needed to keep the law for salvation? Prove your answer. Show from other New Testament passages that salvation does not depend on the works of the law or circumcision.

How was the circumcision problem solved? Who solved it?

If a witness is Spirit-led, will he ever expound a false doctrine? Why is there such a diversity of beliefs held by sincere Christians?

## 17. WITNESSING IN ASIA MINOR AGAIN (15:36–16:10)

36 ¶ And some days after Paul said unto Barnabas, Let us go again and visit our brethren in every city where we have preached the word of the Lord, *and see* how they do.

37 And Barnabas determined to take with them John, whose surname was Mark.

38 But Paul thought not good to take him with them, who departed from them from Pamphylia, and went not with them to the work.

39 And the contention was so sharp between them, that they departed asunder one from the other: and so Barnabas took Mark, and sailed unto Cyprus;

40 And Paul chose Silas, and departed, being recommended by the brethren unto the grace of God.

41 And he went through Syria and Çī-lĭç′-ĭ-ă, confirming the churches.

CHAPTER 16

THEN came he to Dĕr′-bē and Lystra: and, behold, a certain disciple was there, named Tī-mŏth′-ĕ-ŭs, the son of a certain woman, which was a Jewess, and believed; but his father *was* a Greek:

2 Which was well reported of by the brethren that were at Lystra and Ī-cō′-nĭ-ŭm.

3 Him would Paul have to go forth with him; and took and circumcised him because of the Jews which were in those quarters: for they knew all that his father was a Greek.

4 And as they went through the cities, they delivered them the decrees for to keep, that were ordained of the apostles and elders which were at Jerusalem.

5 And so were the churches established in the faith, and increased in number daily.

6 Now when they had gone throughout Phrȳg′-ĭ-ă and the region of Galatia, and were forbidden of the Holy Ghost to preach the word in Asia,

7 After they were come to Mysia, they assayed to go into Bī-thȳn′-ĭ-ă: but the Spirit suffered them not.

8 And they passing by Mysia came down to Trō′-ăs.

9 And a vision appeared to Paul in the night; There stood a man of Macedonia, and prayed him, saying, Come over into Macedonia, and help us.

10 And after he had seen the vision, immediately we endeavoured to go into Macedonia, assuredly gathering that the Lord had called us for to preach the gospel unto them.

Earlier God used persecution to scatter the witnesses. In this passage what did He use to cause two witnessing groups to leave Antioch?

What was the prime reason for this second journey into Asia Minor? Was it valid? Why should a witness "follow up" a convert?

Why did Paul have to have Timothy circumcised, when the church had already decided that circumcision was unnecessary? Was Paul being hypersensitive? Which New Testament principle was Paul possibly thinking of?

From this passage tell why Timothy was selected by Paul to go with him on the witnessing journey (see also I Timothy 4:6 and II Timothy 1:5)?

Does the Holy Spirit ever forbid us to witness? Before you answer too quickly, read the first ten verses of chapter 16. How do we determine who the Holy Spirit wants us to witness to, and when? List clues thus far given in the Book of Acts. Does the Holy Spirit have a witnessing schedule? Did the Holy Spirit ever allow them to witness in Asia? Why, do you think, did He forbid them to go?

## 18. WITNESSING IN MACEDONIA (16:11–17:15)

11 Therefore loosing from Trō′-ăs, we came with a straight course to Săm-ō-thrā′-çi-ă, and the next *day* to Nē-ā′-pŏ-lĭs;

12 And from thence to Phĭ-lĭp′-pī, which is the chief city of that part of Macedonia, *and* a colony: and we were in that city abiding certain days.

13 And on the sabbath we went out of the city by a river side, where prayer was wont to be made; and we sat down, and spake unto the women which resorted *thither*.

14 ¶ And a certain woman named Lydia, a seller of purple, of the city of Thȳ-ă-tī′-ră, which worshipped God, heard *us:* whose heart the Lord opened, that she attended unto the things which were spoken of Paul.

15 And when she was baptized, and her household, she besought *us*, saying, If ye have judged me to be faithful to the Lord, come into my house, and abide *there.* And she constrained us.

16 ¶ And it came to pass, as we went to prayer, a certain damsel

possessed with a spirit of divination met us, which brought her masters much gain by soothsaying:

17 The same followed Paul and us, and cried, saying, These men are the servants of the most high God, which shew unto us the way of salvation.

18 And this did she many days. But Paul, being grieved, turned and said to the spirit, I command thee in the name of Jesus Christ to come out of her. And he came out the same hour.

19 ¶ And when her masters saw that the hope of their gains was gone, they caught Paul and Silas, and drew *them* into the marketplace unto the rulers,

20 And brought them to the magistrates, saying, These men, being Jews, do exceedingly trouble our city,

21 And teach customs, which are not lawful for us to receive, neither to observe, being Romans.

22 And the multitude rose up together against them: and the magistrates rent off their clothes, and commanded to beat *them.*

23 And when they had laid many stripes upon them, they cast *them* into prison, charging the jailer to keep them safely:

24 Who, having received such a charge, thrust them into the inner prison, and made their feet fast in the stocks.

25 ¶ And at midnight Paul and Silas prayed, and sang praises unto God: and the prisoners heard them.

26 And suddenly there was a great earthquake, so that the foundations of the prison were shaken: and immediately all the doors were opened, and every one's bands were loosed.

27 And the keeper of the prison awaking out of his sleep, and seeing the prison doors open, he drew out his sword, and would have killed himself, supposing that the prisoners had been fled.

28 But Paul cried with a loud voice, saying, Do thyself no harm: for we are all here.

29 Then he called for a light, and sprang in, and came trembling, and fell down before Paul and Silas,

30 And brought them out, and said, Sirs, what must I do to be saved?

31 And they said, Believe on the Lord Jesus Christ, and thou shalt be saved, and thy house.

32 And they spake unto him the word of the Lord, and to all that were in his house.

33 And he took them the same hour of the night, and washed *their* stripes; and was baptized, he and all his, straightway.

34 And when he had brought them into his house, he set meat before them, and rejoiced, believing in God with all his house.

35 And when it was day, the magistrates sent the sergeants, saying, Let those men go.

36 And the keeper of the prison told this saying to Paul, The magistrates have sent to let you go: now therefore depart, and go in peace.

37 But Paul said unto them, They have beaten us openly uncondemned, being Romans, and have cast *us* into prison; and now do they thrust us out privily? nay verily; but let them come themselves and fetch us out.

38 And the sergeants told these words unto the magistrates: and they feared, when they heard that they were Romans.

39 And they came and besought them, and brought *them* out, and desired *them* to depart out of the city.

40 And they went out of the prison, and entered into *the house of* Lydia: and when they had seen the brethren, they comforted them, and departed.

## CHAPTER 17

NOW when they had passed through Ăm-phĭp'-ŏ-lĭs and Ăp-ŏl-lō'-nĭ-ă, they came to Thĕss-ă-lō-nī'-că, where was a synagogue of the Jews:

2 And Paul, as his manner was, went in unto them, and three sabbath days reasoned with them out of the scriptures,

3 Opening and alleging, that Christ must needs have suffered, and risen again from the dead; and that this Jesus, whom I preach unto you, is Christ.

4 And some of them believed, and consorted with Paul and Silas; and of the devout Greeks a great multitude, and of the chief women not a few.

5 ¶ But the Jews which believed not, moved with envy, took unto them certain lewd fellows of the baser sort, and gathered a company, and set all the city on an uproar, and assaulted the house of Jason, and sought to bring them out to the people.

6 And when they found them not, they drew Jason and certain brethren unto the rulers of the city, crying, These that have turned the world upside down are come hither also;

7 Whom Jason hath received: and these all do contrary to the decrees of Cæsar, saying that there is another king, *one* Jesus.

8 And they troubled the people and the rulers of the city, when they heard these things.

9 And when they had taken security of Jason, and of the other, they let them go.

10 ¶ And the brethren immediately sent away Paul and Silas by night unto Bĕ-rē′-ă: who coming *thither* went into the synagogue of the Jews.

11 These were more noble than those in Thĕss-ă-lō-nī′-că, in that they received the word with all readiness of mind, and searched the scriptures daily, whether those things were so.

12 Therefore many of them believed; also of honourable women which were Greeks, and of men, not a few.

13 But when the Jews of Thĕss-ă-lō-nī′-că had knowledge that the word of God was preached of Paul at Bĕ-rē′-ă, they came thither also, and stirred up the people.

14 And then immediately the brethren sent away Paul to go as it were to the sea: but Silas and Tī-mŏth′-ĕ-ŭs abode there still.

15 And they that conducted Paul brought him unto Athens: and receiving a commandment unto Silas and Tī-mŏth′-ĕ-ŭs for to come to him with all speed, they departed.

Read very carefully 16:13-15. Was Lydia saved before Paul witnessed to her? Is it possible for a twentieth-century person to be a worshiper of God and not be saved? What is essential for salvation?

Compare the two women that Paul witnessed to at Philippi. What were their similarities? Their differences? From your study of the first fifteen chapters of Acts, recall the people who were converted as the result of a personal witness. What factors in each experience were the same? What were the differences? Notice how different each individual was. Was the same message given? Was it given in the same way? Should our witness message change to appeal to different people?

Compare this witness experience with the one recorded in John 4:1-26. Does the pattern fit both experiences? Apply the pattern to a witnessing experience you had. Does the pattern fit?

Philip's experience is a good example of the combination of "witnessing" and "soul winning." Could soul winning be compared to a salesman's "follow through" or "closing the sale?" If you have concluded that every Christian is a witness for Christ, is everyone a soul winner? Is soul winning a special gift (see Eph. 4:11 and 12)?

While Paul and Silas were in prison at Philippi, they prayed and sang. Is it possible to witness through prayer? Is a silent prayer before a meal in a restaurant a witness? Is it possible to be a witness by singing? Or is singing to be used as the attention-getter? Explain your answer.

Notice that before Paul and Silas had a one-to-one witnessing experience with the jailer, the jailer asked a question. What was it? Should a witness always wait for a question before witnessing one-to-one (I Peter 3:15)? Is a question from an unbeliever an indication of a Spirit-controlled opportunity to witness? In the Book of Acts, are questions asked before the witness message is given? How often does this occur? Why is the Word loved and accepted by some and hated and rejected by others?

# 19. WITNESSING IN GREECE (17:16–18:17)

16 ¶ Now while Paul waited for them at Athens, his spirit was stirred in him, when he saw the city wholly given to idolatry.

17 Therefore disputed he in the synagogue with the Jews, and with the devout persons, and in the market daily with them that met with him.

18 Then certain philosophers of the Ĕp-ĭ-cū-rē′-ăns, and of the Stō′-ĭcs, encountered him. And some said, What will this babbler say? other some, He seemeth to be a setter forth of strange gods: because he preached unto them Jesus and the resurrection.

19 And they took him, and brought him unto Ăr-ĕ-ŏp′-ă-gŭs, saying, May we know what this new doctrine, whereof thou speakest, *is?*

20 For thou bringest certain strange things to our ears: we would know therefore what these things mean.

21 (For all the Athenians and strangers which were there spent their time in nothing else, but either to tell, or to hear some new thing.)

22 ¶ Then Paul stood in the midst of Mars' hill, and said, *Ye* men of Athens, I perceive that in all things ye are too superstitious.

23 For as I passed by, and beheld your devotions, I found an altar with this inscription, TO THE UNKNOWN GOD. Whom therefore ye ignorantly worship, him declare I unto you.

24 God that made the world and all things therein, seeing that he is Lord of heaven and earth, dwelleth not in temples made with hands;

25 Neither is worshipped with men's hands, as though he needed any thing, seeing he giveth to all life, and breath, and all things;

26 And hath made of one blood all nations of men for to dwell on all the face of the earth, and hath determined the times before appointed, and the bounds of their habitation;

27 That they should seek the Lord, if haply they might feel after him, and find him, though he be not far from every one of us:

28 For in him we live, and move, and have our being; as certain also of your own poets have said, For we are also his offspring.

29 Forasmuch then as we are the offspring of God, we ought not to think that the Godhead is like unto gold, or silver, or stone, graven by art and man's device.

30 And the times of this ignorance God winked at; but now commandeth all men everywhere to repent:

31 Because he hath appointed a day, in the which he will judge the world in righteousness by *that* man whom he hath ordained; *whereof* he hath given assurance unto all *men*, in that he hath raised him from the dead.

32 ¶ And when they heard of the resurrection of the dead, some mocked: and others said, We will hear thee again of this *matter*.

33 So Paul departed from among them.

34 Howbeit certain men clave unto him, and believed: among the which *was* Dī-ō-nȳs′-ĭ-ŭs the Ăr-ĕ-ŏp′-ă-gīte, and a woman named Dăm′-ă-rĭs, and others with them.

## CHAPTER 18

AFTER these things Paul departed from Athens, and came to Corinth;

2 And found a certain Jew named Aquila, born in Pontus, lately come from Italy, with his wife Priscilla; (because that Claudius had commanded all Jews to depart from Rome:) and came unto them.

3 And because he was of the same craft, he abode with them, and wrought: for by their occupation they were tentmakers.

4 And he reasoned in the synagogue every sabbath, and persuaded the Jews and the Greeks.

5 And when Silas and Tī-mŏth′-ĕ-ŭs were come from Macedonia,

Paul was pressed in the spirit, and testified to the Jews *that* Jesus *was* Christ.

6 And when they opposed themselves, and blasphemed, he shook *his* raiment, and said unto them, Your blood *be* upon your own heads; I *am* clean: from henceforth I will go unto the Gentiles.

7 And he departed thence, and entered into a certain *man's* house, named Justus, *one* that worshipped God, whose house joined hard to the synagogue.

8 And Crispus, the chief ruler of the synagogue, believed on the Lord with all his house; and many of the Corinthians hearing believed, and were baptized.

9 Then spake the Lord to Paul in the night by a vision, Be not afraid, but speak, and hold not thy peace:

10 For I am with thee, and no man shall set on thee to hurt thee: for I have much people in this city.

11 And he continued *there* a year and six months, teaching the word of God among them.

12 ¶ And when Găl'-lĭ-ō was the deputy of Ă-chā̂i'-ă, the Jews made insurrection with one accord against Paul, and brought him to the judgment seat,

13 Saying, This *fellow* persuadeth men to worship God contrary to the law.

14 And when Paul was now about to open *his* mouth, Găl'-lĭ-ō said unto the Jews, If it were a matter of wrong or wicked lewdness, O *ye* Jews, reason would that I should bear with you:

15 But if it be a question of words and names, and *of* your law, look ye *to it;* for I will be no

16 And he drave them from the judgment seat.

17 Then all the Greeks took Sŏs'-thĕ-nēs, the chief ruler of the synagogue, and beat *him* before the judgment seat. And Găl'-lĭ-ō cared for none of those things.

This was the first time that Paul had visited Athens. Using the above passage, describe the setting and the people. Why was Paul distressed?

Paul witnessed for Christ in the synagogue and in the marketplace. With what type of people did he converse in the synagogue? In the marketplace? Why did both types need Christ?

Looking back through the Book of Acts, in what different kinds of places did the witnesses witness? Is there any place where a witness cannot be given? Why, or why not?

Describe the types of people Paul witnessed to thus far. Illustrate the different approaches or openings he used. Even though Paul witnessed to a wide variety of people, his basic message was the same. Why? Point out the core of the witness message to the Athenians.

How did Paul gain the attention of the philosophers? Notice the question in verse 19. Learn to listen for the question that can lead to an opportunity to witness.

Two people are named in verse 34. Are their names mentioned again in the New Testament? Why is it important to remember a person's name? List the individual names of those who came to Christ mentioned in the Book of Acts. What does this tell about the importance of the individual person to Christ?

Paul was in Athens for over a year. Shouldn't he have covered more territory? Was he still being guided by the Holy Spirit? What were the results? Are results an indication of being led by the Holy Spirit? Does God still lead us directly in witnessing today? Explain your answer.

## 20. WITNESSING IN ASIA (18:18–20:38)

18 ¶ And Paul *after this* tarried *there* yet a good while, and then took his leave of the brethren, and sailed thence into Syria, and with him Priscilla and Aquila; having shorn *his* head in Cĕn-chrē′-ă: for he had a vow.

19 And he came to Ephesus, and left them there: but he himself entered into the synagogue, and reasoned with the Jews.

20 When they desired *him* to tarry longer time with them, he consented not;

21 But bade them farewell, saying, I must by all means keep this feast that cometh in Jerusalem: but I will return again unto you, if God will. And he sailed from Ephesus.

22 And when he had landed at Cæsarea, and gone up, and saluted the church, he went down to Ăn′-tĭ-ŏch.

23 And after he had spent some time *there,* he departed, and went over *all* the country of Galatia and Phrÿġ′-ĭ-ă in order, strengthening all the disciples.

24 ¶ And a certain Jew named Ă-pŏl′-lŏs, born at Alexandria, an eloquent man, *and* mighty in the scriptures, came to Ephesus.

25 This man was instructed in the way of the Lord; and being fervent in the spirit, he spake and taught diligently the things of the Lord, knowing only the baptism of John.

26 And he began to speak boldly in the synagogue: whom when Aquila and Priscilla had heard,

they took him unto *them*, and expounded unto him the way of God more perfectly.

27 And when he was disposed to pass into Ă-chā̂ī′-ă, the brethren wrote, exhorting the disciples to receive him: who, when he was come, helped them much which had believed through grace:

28 For he mightily convinced the Jews, *and that* publicly, shewing by the scriptures that Jesus was Christ.

## CHAPTER 19

AND it came to pass, that, while Ă-pŏl′-lŏs was at Corinth, Paul having passed through the upper coasts came to Ephesus: and finding certain disciples,

2 He said unto them, Have ye received the Holy Ghost since ye believed? And they said unto him, We have not so much as heard whether there be any Holy Ghost.

3 And he said unto them, Unto what then were ye baptized? And they said, Unto John's baptism.

4 Then said Paul, John verily baptized with the baptism of repentance, saying unto the people, that they should believe on him which should come after him, that is, on Christ Jesus.

5 When they heard *this*, they were baptized in the name of the Lord Jesus.

6 And when Paul had laid *his* hands upon them, the Holy Ghost came on them; and they spake with tongues, and prophesied.

7 And all the men were about twelve.

8 And he went into the synagogue, and spake boldly for the space of three months, disputing and persuading the things concerning the kingdom of God.

9 But when divers were hardened, and believed not, but spake evil of that way before the multitude, he departed from them, and separated the disciples, disputing daily in the school of one Tyrannus.

10 And this continued by the space of two years; so that all they which dwelt in Asia heard the word of the Lord Jesus, both Jews and Greeks.

11 And God wrought special miracles by the hands of Paul:

12 So that from his body were brought unto the sick handkerchiefs or aprons, and the diseases departed from them, and the evil spirits went out of them.

13 ¶ Then certain of the vagabond Jews, exorcists, took upon them to call over them which had evil spirits the name of the Lord Jesus, saying, We adjure you by Jesus whom Paul preacheth.

14 And there were seven sons of *one* Sçē′-vă, a Jew, *and* chief of the priests, which did so.

15 And the evil spirit answered and said, Jesus I know, and Paul I know; but who are ye?

16 And the man in whom the evil spirit was leaped on them, and overcame them, and prevailed against them, so that they fled out of that house naked and wounded.

17 And this was known to all the Jews and Greeks also dwelling at Ephesus; and fear fell on them all, and the name of the Lord Jesus was magnified.

18 And many that believed came, and confessed, and shewed their deeds.

19 Many of them also which used curious arts brought their books together, and burned them before all *men:* and they counted the price of them, and found *it* fifty thousand *pieces* of silver.

20 So mightily grew the word of God and prevailed.

21 ¶ After these things were ended, Paul purposed in the spirit, when he had passed through Macedonia and Ă-chā̂ī′-ă, to go to Jerusalem, saying, After I have been there, I must also see Rome.

22 So he sent into Macedonia two of them that ministered unto him, Tī-mŏth′-ĕ-ŭs and Erastus; but he himself stayed in Asia for a season.

23 And the same time there arose no small stir about that way.

24 For a certain *man* named Dē-mē′-trĭ-ŭs, a silversmith, which

made silver shrines for Diana, brought no small gain unto the craftsmen;

25 Whom he called together with the workmen of like occupation, and said, Sirs, ye know that by this craft we have our wealth.

26 Moreover ye see and hear, that not alone at Ephesus, but almost throughout all Asia, this Paul hath persuaded and turned away much people, saying that they be no gods, which are made with hands:

27 So that not only this our craft is in danger to be set at nought; but also that the temple of the great goddess Diana should be despised, and her magnificence should be destroyed, whom all Asia and the world worshippeth.

28 And when they heard *these sayings*, they were full of wrath, and cried out, saying, Great *is* Diana of the Ephesians.

29 And the whole city was filled with confusion: and having caught Gâi′-ŭs and Ăr-ĭs-tär′-chŭs, men of Macedonia, Paul's companions in travel, they rushed with one accord into the theatre.

30 And when Paul would have entered in unto the people, the disciples suffered him not.

31 And certain of the chief of Asia, which were his friends, sent unto him, desiring *him* that he would not adventure himself into the theatre.

32 Some therefore cried one thing, and some another: for the assembly was confused; and the more part knew not wherefore they were come together.

33 And they drew Alexander out of the multitude, the Jews putting him forward. And Alexander beckoned with the hand, and would have made his defence unto the people.

34 But when they knew that he was a Jew, all with one voice about the space of two hours cried out, Great *is* Diana of the Ephesians.

35 And when the townclerk had appeased the people, he said, *Ye* men of Ephesus, what man is there that knoweth not how that the city of the Ephesians is a worshipper of the great goddess Diana, and of the *image* which fell down from Jupiter?

36 Seeing then that these things cannot be spoken against, ye ought to be quiet, and to do nothing rashly.

37 For ye have brought hither these men, which are neither robbers of churches, nor yet blasphemers of your goddess.

38 Wherefore if Dē-mē′-trĭ-ŭs, and the craftsmen which are with him, have a matter against any man, the law is open, and there are deputies: let them implead one another.

39 But if ye inquire any thing concerning other matters, it shall be determined in a lawful assembly.

40 For we are in danger to be called in question for this day's uproar, there being no cause whereby we may give an account of this concourse.

41 And when he had thus spoken, he dismissed the assembly.

## CHAPTER 20

AND after the uproar was ceased, Paul called unto *him* the disciples, and embraced *them*, and departed for to go into Macedonia.

2 And when he had gone over those parts, and had given them much exhortation, he came into Greece,

3 And *there* abode three months. And when the Jews laid wait for him, as he was about to sail into Syria, he purposed to return through Macedonia.

4 And there accompanied him into Asia Sō′-pă-tĕr of Bĕ-rē′-ă; and of the Thĕss-ă-lō′-nĭ-ăns, Ăr-ĭs-tär′-chŭs and Sĕ-cŭn′-dŭs; and Gâi′-ŭs of Dĕr′-bē, and Tĭ-mŏth′-ĕ-ŭs; and of Asia, Tȳch′-ĭ-cŭs and Trŏph′-ĭ-mŭs.

5 These going before tarried for us at Trō′-ăs.

6 And we sailed away from Phĭ-lĭp′-pī after the days of unleavened bread, and came unto them to Trō′-ăs in five days; where we abode seven days.

7 And upon the first *day* of the week, when the disciples came together to break bread, Paul preached unto them, ready to depart on the morrow; and continued his speech until midnight.

8 And there were many lights in the upper chamber, where they were gathered together.

9 And there sat in a window a certain young man named Eû'-tў-chŭs, being fallen into a deep sleep: and as Paul was long preaching, he sunk down with sleep, and fell down from the third loft, and was taken up dead.

10 And Paul went down, and fell on him, and embracing *him* said, Trouble not yourselves; for his life is in him.

11 When he therefore was come up again, and had broken bread, and eaten, and talked a long while, even till break of day, so he departed.

12 And they brought the young man alive, and were not a little comforted.

13 ¶ And we went before to ship, and sailed unto Assos, there intending to take in Paul: for so had he appointed, minding himself to go afoot.

14 And when he met with us at Assos, we took him in, and came to Mĭt-ў-lē'-nē.

15 And we sailed thence, and came the next *day* over against Chī'-ŏs; and the next *day* we arrived at Samos, and tarried at Trō-gўl'-lĭ-ŭm; and the next *day* we came to Mī-lē'-tŭs.

16 For Paul had determined to sail by Ephesus, because he would not spend the time in Asia: for he hasted, if it were possible for him, to be at Jerusalem the day of Pentecost.

17 ¶ And from Mī-lē'-tŭs he sent to Ephesus, and called the elders of the church.

18 And when they were come to him, he said unto them, Ye know, from the first day that I came into Asia, after what manner I have been with you at all seasons,

19 Serving the Lord with all humility of mind, and with many tears, and temptations, which befell me by the lying in wait of the Jews:

20 *And* how I kept back nothing that was profitable *unto you,* but have shewed you, and have taught you publicly, and from house to house,

21 Testifying both to the Jews, and also to the Greeks, repentance toward God, and faith toward our Lord Jesus Christ.

22 And now, behold, I go bound in the spirit unto Jerusalem, not knowing the things that shall befall me there:

23 Save that the Holy Ghost witnesseth in every city, saying that bonds and afflictions abide me.

24 But none of these things move me, neither count I my life dear unto myself, so that I might finish my course with joy, and the ministry, which I have received of the Lord Jesus, to testify the gospel of the grace of God.

25 And now, behold, I know that ye all, among whom I have gone preaching the kingdom of God, shall see my face no more.

26 Wherefore I take you to record this day, that I *am* pure from the blood of all *men.*

27 For I have not shunned to declare unto you all the counsel of God.

28 ¶ Take heed therefore unto yourselves, and to all the flock, over the which the Holy Ghost hath made you overseers, to feed the church of God, which he hath purchased with his own blood.

29 For I know this, that after my departing shall grievous wolves enter in among you, not sparing the flock.

30 Also of your own selves shall men arise, speaking perverse things, to draw away disciples after them.

31 Therefore watch, and remember, that by the space of three years I ceased not to warn every one night and day with tears.

32 And now, brethren, I commend you to God, and to the word of his grace, which is able to build you up, and to give you an inheritance among all them which are sanctified.

33 I have coveted no man's silver, or gold, or apparel.

34 Yea, ye yourselves know, that these hands have ministered unto my necessities, and to them that were with me.

35 I have shewed you all things, how that so labouring ye ought to support the weak, and to remember the words of the Lord Jesus, how he said, It is more blessed to give than to receive.

36 ¶ And when he had thus spoken, he kneeled down, and prayed with them all.

37 And they all wept sore, and fell on Paul's neck, and kissed him,

38 Sorrowing most of all for the words which he spake, that they should see his face no more. And they accompanied him unto the ship.

List the names of the witnesses mentioned in this passage. Note the chain reaction in witnessing and the training of witnesses. Prove from this passage that witnesses need growth and training.

What was Apollo's unusual gift?

List some of the things accomplished by Paul during his two years in Ephesus.

This passage says that Paul had discussions (or witnessed) daily in the lecture hall of Tyrannus. How do you account for the fact that every Jew and Greek living in Asia heard the Word of the Lord (12:10)? Compare our medias for witnessing with those in Paul's time.

In verse 20 the phrase is used again: "So mightily grew the word of God . . ." How could the Word of God grow in power (see vv. 17-20)? Read this passage from The International Version of the New Testament.

What effect did the witnesses have on their community? How can this encourage today's witnesses for Christ?

Paul became personally involved with his converts. List specific phrases used to describe that involvement (chap.

20). What does that say to twentieth-century witnesses? The persecution and trouble that followed the witnesses has already been discussed. What were some of the benefits the witnesses received (chap. 20)? Share some blessings you received from a recent witnessing experience.

## 21. WITNESSING IN JERUSALEM AGAIN (21:1–23:35)

### CHAPTER 21

AND it came to pass, that after we were gotten from them, and had launched, we came with a straight course unto Cō′-ŏs, and the *day* following unto Rhodes, and from thence unto Patara:

2 And finding a ship sailing over unto Phē-nīç′-ịă, we went aboard, and set forth.

3 Now when we had discovered Cyprus, we left it on the left hand, and sailed into Syria, and landed at Tyre: for there the ship was to unlade her burden.

4 And finding disciples, we tarried there seven days: who said to Paul through the Spirit, that he should not go up to Jerusalem.

5 And when we had accomplished those days, we departed and went our way; and they all brought us on our way, with wives and children, till *we were* out of the city: and we kneeled down on the shore, and prayed.

6 And when we had taken our leave one of another, we took ship; and they returned home again.

7 And when we had finished *our* course from Tyre, we came to Ptŏl-ĕ-mā′-ĭs, and saluted the brethren, and abode with them one day.

8 And the next *day* we that were of Paul's company departed, and came unto Cæsarea: and we entered into the house of Philip the evangelist, which was *one* of the seven; and abode with him.

9 And the same man had four daughters, virgins, which did prophesy.

10 And as we tarried *there* many days, there came down from Judæa a certain prophet, named Ăg′-ă-bŭs.

11 And when he was come unto us, he took Paul's girdle, and bound his own hands and feet, and said, Thus saith the Holy Ghost, So shall the Jews at Jerusalem bind the man that owneth this girdle, and shall deliver *him* into the hands of the Gentiles.

12 And when we heard these things, both we, and they of that place, besought him not to go up to Jerusalem.

13 Then Paul answered, What mean ye to weep and to break mine heart? for I am ready not to be bound only, but also to die at Jerusalem for the name of the Lord Jesus.

14 And when he would not be persuaded, we ceased, saying, The will of the Lord be done.

15 And after those days we took up our carriages, and went up to Jerusalem.

16 There went with us also *certain* of the disciples of Cæsarea, and brought with them one Mnā′-sọn of Cyprus, an old disciple, with whom we should lodge.

17 And when we were come to Jerusalem, the brethren received us gladly.

18 And the *day* following Paul went in with us unto James; and all the elders were present.

19 And when he had saluted them, he declared particularly what things God had wrought among the Gentiles by his ministry.

20 And when they heard *it*, they glorified the Lord, and said unto him, Thou seest, brother, how many thousands of Jews there are which believe; and they are all zealous of the law:

21 And they are informed of thee, that thou teachest all the Jews which are among the Gentiles to forsake Moses, saying that they ought not to circumcise *their* children, neither to walk after the customs.

22 What is it therefore? the multitude must needs come together: for they will hear that thou art come.

23 Do therefore this that we say to thee: We have four men which have a vow on them;

24 Them take, and purify thyself with them, and be at charges with them, that they may shave *their* heads: and all may know that those things, whereof they were informed concerning thee, are nothing; but *that* thou thyself also walkest orderly, and keepest the law.

25 As touching the Gentiles which believe, we have written *and* concluded that they observe no such thing, save only that they keep themselves from *things* offered to idols, and from blood, and from strangled, and from fornication.

26 Then Paul took the men, and the next day purifying himself with them entered into the temple, to signify the accomplishment of the days of purification, until that an offering should be offered for every one of them.

27 And when the seven days were almost ended, the Jews which were of Asia, when they saw him in the temple, stirred up all the people, and laid hands on him,

28 Crying out, Men of Israel, help: This is the man, that teacheth all *men* every where against the people, and the law, and this place: and further brought Greeks also into the temple, and hath polluted this holy place.

29 (For they had seen before with him in the city Trŏph′-ĭ-mŭs an Ephesian, whom they supposed that Paul had brought into the temple.)

30 And all the city was moved, and the people ran together: and they took Paul, and drew him out of the temple: and forthwith the doors were shut.

31 And as they went about to kill him, tidings came unto the chief captain of the band, that all Jerusalem was in an uproar.

32 Who immediately took soldiers and centurions, and ran down unto them: and when they saw the chief captain and the soldiers, they left beating of Paul.

33 Then the chief captain came near, and took him, and commanded *him* to be bound with two chains; and demanded who he was, and what he had done.

34 And some cried one thing, some another, among the multitude: and when he could not know the certainty for the tumult, he commanded him to be carried into the castle.

35 And when he came upon the stairs, so it was, that he was borne of the soldiers for the violence of the people.

36 For the multitude of the people followed after, crying, Away with him.

37 And as Paul was to be led into the castle, he said unto the chief captain, May I speak unto thee? Who said, Canst thou speak Greek?

38 Art not thou that Egyptian, which before these days madest an uproar, and leddest out into the wilderness four thousand men that were murderers?

39 But Paul said, I am a man *which am* a Jew of Tarsus, *a city* in Çĭ-lĭç′-ĭ-ă, a citizen of no mean city: and, I beseech thee, suffer me to speak unto the people.

40 And when he had given him licence, Paul stood on the stairs, and beckoned with the hand unto the people. And when there was made a great silence, he spake unto *them* in the Hebrew tongue,

## CHAPTER 22

MEN, brethren, and fathers, hear ye my defence *which I make* now unto you.

2 (And when they heard that he spake in the Hebrew tongue to them, they kept the more silence: and he saith,)

3 I am verily a man *which am* a Jew, born in Tarsus, *a city* in Cĭ-lĭç'-ĭ-ă, yet brought up in this city at the feet of Gă-mā'-lĭ-ĕl, *and* taught according to the perfect manner of the law of the fathers, and was zealous toward God, as ye all are this day.

4 And I persecuted this way unto the death, binding and delivering into prisons both men and women.

5 As also the high priest doth bear me witness, and all the estate of the elders: from whom also I received letters unto the brethren, and went to Damascus, to bring them which were there bound unto Jerusalem, for to be punished.

6 And it came to pass, that, as I made my journey, and was come nigh unto Damascus about noon, suddenly there shone from heaven a great light round about me.

7 And I fell unto the ground, and heard a voice saying unto me, Saul, Saul, why persecutest thou me?

8 And I answered, Who art thou, Lord? And he said unto me, I am Jesus of Nazareth, whom thou persecutest.

9 And they that were with me saw indeed the light, and were afraid; but they heard not the voice of him that spake to me.

10 And I said, What shall I do, Lord? And the Lord said unto me, Arise, and go into Damascus; and there it shall be told thee of all things which are appointed for thee to do.

11 And when I could not see for the glory of that light, being led by the hand of them that were with me, I came into Damascus.

12 And one Ăn-ă-nī'-ăs, a devout man according to the law, having a good report of all the Jews which dwelt *there*,

13 Came unto me, and stood, and said unto me, Brother Saul, receive thy sight. And the same hour I looked up upon him.

14 And he said, The God of our fathers hath chosen thee, that thou shouldest know his will, and see that Just One, and shouldest hear the voice of his mouth.

15 For thou shalt be his witness unto all men of what thou hast seen and heard.

16 And now why tarriest thou? arise, and be baptized, and wash away thy sins, calling on the name of the Lord.

17 And it came to pass, that, when I was come again to Jerusalem, even while I prayed in the temple, I was in a trance;

18 And saw him saying unto me, Make haste, and get thee quickly out of Jerusalem: for they will not receive thy testimony concerning me.

19 And I said, Lord, they know that I imprisoned and beat in every synagogue them that believed on thee:

20 And when the blood of thy martyr Stephen was shed, I also was standing by, and consenting unto his death, and kept the raiment of them that slew him.

21 And he said unto me, Depart: for I will send thee far hence unto the Gentiles.

22 And they gave him audience unto this word, and *then* lifted up their voices, and said, Away with such a *fellow* from the earth: for it is not fit that he should live.

23 And as they cried out, and cast off *their* clothes, and threw dust into the air,

24 The chief captain commanded him to be brought into the castle, and bade that he should be examined by scourging; that he might know wherefore they cried so against him.

25 And as they bound him with thongs, Paul said unto the centurion that stood by, Is it lawful for you to scourge a man that is a Roman, and uncondemned?

26 When the centurion heard *that*, he went and told the chief captain, saying, Take heed what thou doest: for this man is a Roman.

27 Then the chief captain came, and said unto him, Tell me, art thou a Roman? He said, Yea.
28 And the chief captain answered, With a great sum obtained I this freedom. And Paul said, But I was *free* born.
29 Then straightway they departed from him which should have examined him: and the chief captain also was afraid, after he knew that he was a Roman, and because he had bound him.
30 On the morrow, because he would have known the certainty wherefore he was accused of the Jews, he loosed him from *his* bands, and commanded the chief priests and all their council to appear, and brought Paul down, and set him before them.

## CHAPTER 23

AND Paul, earnestly beholding the council, said, Men *and* brethren, I have lived in all good conscience before God until this day.
2 And the high priest Ăn-ă-nī'-ăs commanded them that stood by him to smite him on the mouth.
3 Then said Paul unto him, God shall smite thee, *thou* whited wall: for sittest thou to judge me after the law, and commandest me to be smitten contrary to the law?
4 And they that stood by said, Revilest thou God's high priest?
5 Then said Paul, I wist not, brethren, that he was the high priest: for it is written, Thou shalt not speak evil of the ruler of thy people.
6 But when Paul perceived that the one part were Sadducees, and the other Pharisees, he cried out in the council, Men *and* brethren, I am a Pharisee, the son of a Pharisee: of the hope and resurrection of the dead I am called in question.
7 And when he had so said, there arose a dissension between the Pharisees and the Sadducees: and the multitude was divided.
8 For the Sadducees say that there is no resurrection, neither angel, nor spirit: but the Pharisees confess both.
9 And there arose a great cry: and the scribes *that were* of the Pharisees' part arose, and strove, saying, We find no evil in this man: but if a spirit or an angel hath spoken to him, let us not fight against God.
10 And when there arose a great dissension, the chief captain, fearing lest Paul should have been pulled in pieces of them, commanded the soldiers to go down, and to take him by force from among them, and to bring *him* into the castle.
11 And the night following the Lord stood by him, and said, Be of good cheer, Paul: for as thou hast testified of me in Jerusalem, so must thou bear witness also at Rome.
12 And when it was day, certain of the Jews banded together, and bound themselves under a curse, saying that they would neither eat nor drink till they had killed Paul.
13 And they were more than forty which had made this conspiracy.
14 And they came to the chief priests and elders, and said, We have bound ourselves under a great curse, that we will eat nothing until we have slain Paul.
15 Now therefore ye with the council signify to the chief captain that he bring him down unto you to-morrow, as though ye would inquire something more perfectly concerning him: and we, or ever he come near, are ready to kill him.
16 And when Paul's sister's son heard of their lying in wait, he went and entered into the castle, and told Paul.
17 Then Paul called one of the centurions unto *him*, and said, Bring this young man unto the chief captain: for he hath a certain thing to tell him.
18 So he took him, and brought *him* to the chief captain, and said, Paul the prisoner called me unto *him*, and prayed me to bring this young man unto thee, who hath something to say unto thee.
19 Then the chief captain took

him by the hand, and went *with him* aside privately, and asked *him*, What is that thou hast to tell me?

20 And he said, The Jews have agreed to desire thee that thou wouldest bring down Paul tomorrow into the council, as though they would inquire somewhat of him more perfectly.

21 But do not thou yield unto them: for there lie in wait for him of them more than forty men, which have bound themselves with an oath, that they will neither eat nor drink till they have killed him: and now are they ready, looking for a promise from thee.

22 So the chief captain *then* let the young man depart, and charged *him*, *See thou* tell no man that thou hast shewed these things to me.

23 And he called unto *him* two centurions, saying, Make ready two hundred soldiers to go to Cæsarea, and horsemen threescore and ten, and spearmen two hundred, at the third hour of the night;

24 And provide *them* beasts, that they may set Paul on, and bring *him* safe unto Felix the governor.

25 And he wrote a letter after this manner:

26 Claudius Lȳs′-ĭ-ăs unto the most excellent governor Felix *sendeth* greeting.

27 This man was taken of the Jews, and should have been killed of them: then came I with an army, and rescued him, having understood that he was a Roman.

28 And when I would have known the cause wherefore they accused him, I brought him forth into their council:

29 Whom I perceived to be accused of questions of their law, but to have nothing laid to his charge worthy of death or of bonds.

30 And when it was told me how that the Jews laid wait for the man, I sent straightway to thee, and gave commandment to his accusers also to say before thee what *they had* against him. Farewell.

31 Then the soldiers, as it was commanded them, took Paul, and brought *him* by night to Ăn-tĭp′-ă-trĭs.

32 On the morrow they left the horsemen to go with him, and returned to the castle:

33 Who, when they came to Cæsarea, and delivered the epistle to the governor, presented Paul also before him.

34 And when the governor had read *the letter*, he asked of what province he was. And when he understood that *he was* of Çĭ-lĭç′-ĭ-ă;

35 I will hear thee, said he, when thine accusers are also come. And he commanded him to be kept in Herod's judgment hall.

Paul traveled several thousand miles during his lifetime. What two purposes did he accomplish on these trips? Has travel given you an opportunity to witness for Christ? What precautions need to be taken? Why is it easier to witness to a stranger than to a friend? What specifically can be done to overcome reticence to witness to close friends and relatives?

Describe the problem Paul faced when he returned to

Jerusalem. Why were the Jews so sensitive about this point? Describe the solution offered and the events that occurred when Paul followed the advice given him.

In what ways is Paul's defense (chap. 22) a good witnessing message? Why was there such a violent reaction to his message?

To whom does Paul witness in 23:1-9? How did this message vary from previous messages? Was this a clear witness, or did it only serve the purpose of dividing the people who heard it? Explain your answer.

What promise did Paul receive from God in 23:11? List promises that twentieth-century witnesses have.

How do the events in 23:12-35 fit in with God's plan that Paul would witness for Him in Rome?

## 22. WITNESSING IN CAESAREA (24:1–26:32)

CHAPTER 24

AND after five days Ăn-ă-nī'-ăs the high priest descended with the elders, and *with* a certain orator *named* Tĕr-tŭl'-lŭs, who informed the governor against Paul.

2 And when he was called forth, Tĕr-tŭl'-lŭs began to accuse *him*, saying, Seeing that by thee we enjoy great quietness, and that very worthy deeds are done unto this nation by thy providence,

3 We accept *it* always, and in all places, most noble Felix, with all thankfulness.

4 Notwithstanding, that I be not further tedious unto thee, I pray thee that thou wouldest hear us of thy clemency a few words.

5 For we have found this man *a* pestilent *fellow*, and a mover of sedition among all the Jews throughout the world, and a ringleader of the sect of the Nazarenes:

6 Who also hath gone about to profane the temple: whom we took, and would have judged according to our law.

7 But the chief captain Lȳs'-ĭ-ăs came *upon us*, and with great violence took *him* away out of our hands,

8 Commanding his accusers to come unto thee: by examining of whom thyself mayest take knowl-

edge of all these things, whereof we accuse him.

9 And the Jews also assented, saying that these things were so.

10 Then Paul, after that the governor had beckoned unto him to speak, answered, Forasmuch as I know that thou hast been of many years a judge unto this nation, I do the more cheerfully answer for myself:

11 Because that thou mayest understand, that there are yet but twelve days since I went up to Jerusalem for to worship.

12 And they neither found me in the temple disputing with any man, neither raising up the people, neither in the synagogues, nor in the city:

13 Neither can they prove the things whereof they now accuse me.

14 But this I confess unto thee, that after the way which they call heresy, so worship I the God of my fathers, believing all things which are written in the law and in the prophets:

15 And have hope toward God, which they themselves also allow, that there shall be a resurrection of the dead, both of the just and unjust.

16 And herein do I exercise myself, to have always a conscience void of offence toward God, and *toward* men.

17 Now after many years I came to bring alms to my nation, and offerings.

18 Whereupon certain Jews from Asia found me purified in the temple, neither with multitude, nor with tumult.

19 Who ought to have been here before thee, and object, if they had aught against me.

20 Or else let these same *here* say, if they have found any evil doing in me, while I stood before the council,

21 Except it be for this one voice, that I cried standing among them, Touching the resurrection of the dead I am called in question by you this day.

22 And when Felix heard these things, having more perfect knowledge of *that* way, he deferred them, and said, When Lȳs′-ĭ-ăs the chief captain shall come down, I will know the uttermost of your matter.

23 And he commanded a centurion to keep Paul, and to let *him* have liberty, and that he should forbid none of his acquaintance to minister or come unto him.

24 And after certain days, when Felix came with his wife Drŭ-sĭl′-lă, which was a Jewess, he sent for Paul, and heard him concerning the faith in Christ.

25 And as he reasoned of righteousness, temperance, and judgment to come, Felix trembled, and answered, Go thy way for this time; when I have a convenient season, I will call for thee.

26 He hoped also that money should have been given him of Paul, that he might loose him: wherefore he sent for him the oftener, and communed with him.

27 But after two years Pôr′-çĭ-ŭs Festus came into Felix' room: and Felix, willing to shew the Jews a pleasure, left Paul bound.

## CHAPTER 25

NOW when Festus was come into the province, after three days he ascended from Cæsarea to Jerusalem.

2 Then the high priest and the chief of the Jews informed him against Paul, and besought him,

3 And desired favour against him, that he would send for him to Jerusalem, laying wait in the way to kill him.

4 But Festus answered, that Paul should be kept at Cæsarea, and that he himself would depart shortly *thither*.

5 Let them therefore, said he, which among you are able, go down with *me*, and accuse this man, if there be any wickedness in him.

6 And when he had tarried among them more than ten days, he went down unto Cæsarea; and the next day sitting on the judgment seat commanded Paul to be brought.

7 And when he was come, the Jews which came down from Jerusalem stood round about, and laid many and grievous complaints against Paul, which they could not prove.

8 While he answered for himself, Neither against the law of the Jews, neither against the temple, nor yet against Cæsar, have I offended any thing at all.

9 But Festus, willing to do the Jews a pleasure, answered Paul, and said, Wilt thou go up to Jerusalem, and there be judged of these things before me?

10 Then said Paul, I stand at Cæsar's judgment seat, where I ought to be judged: to the Jews have I done no wrong, as thou very well knowest.

11 For if I be an offender, or have committed any thing worthy of death, I refuse not to die: but if there be none of these things whereof these accuse me, no man may deliver me unto them. I appeal unto Cæsar.

12 Then Festus, when he had conferred with the council, answered, Hast thou appealed unto Cæsar? unto Cæsar shalt thou go.

13 And after certain days king Ă-grĭp′-pă and Bĕr-nī′-çē came unto Cæsarea to salute Festus.

14 And when they had been there many days, Festus declared Paul's cause unto the king, saying, There is a certain man left in bonds by Felix:

15 About whom, when I was at Jerusalem, the chief priests and the elders of the Jews informed *me*, desiring *to have* judgment against him.

16 To whom I answered, It is not the manner of the Romans to deliver any man to die, before that he which is accused have the accusers face to face, and have licence to answer for himself concerning the crime laid against him.

17 Therefore, when they were come hither, without any delay on the morrow I sat on the judgment seat, and commanded the man to be brought forth.

18 Against whom when the accusers stood up, they brought none accusation of such things as I supposed:

19 But had certain questions against him of their own superstition, and of one Jesus, which was dead, whom Paul affirmed to be alive.

20 And because I doubted of such manner of questions, I asked *him* whether he would go to Jerusalem, and there be judged of these matters.

21 But when Paul had appealed to be reserved unto the hearing of Augustus, I commanded him to be kept till I might send him to Cæsar.

22 Then Ă-grĭp′-pă said unto Festus, I would also hear the man myself. To-morrow, said he, thou shalt hear him.

23 And on the morrow, when Ă-grĭp′-pă was come, and Bĕr-nī′-çē, with great pomp, and was entered into the place of hearing, with the chief captains, and principal men of the city, at Festus' commandment Paul was brought forth.

24 And Festus said, King Ă-grĭp′-pă, and all men which are here present with us, ye see this man, about whom all the multitude of the Jews have dealt with me, both at Jerusalem, and *also* here, crying that he ought not to live any longer.

25 But when I found that he had committed nothing worthy of death, and that he himself hath appealed to Augustus, I have determined to send him.

26 Of whom I have no certain thing to write unto my lord. Wherefore I have brought him forth before you, and specially before thee, O king Ă-grĭp′-pă, that, after examination had, I might have somewhat to write.

27 For it seemeth to me unreasonable to send a prisoner, and not withal to signify the crimes *laid* against him.

## CHAPTER 26

THEN Ă-grĭp′-pă said unto Paul, Thou art permitted to speak for thyself. Then Paul stretched forth the hand, and answered for himself:

2 I think myself happy, king Ā-grĭp′-pă, because I shall answer for myself this day before thee touching all the things whereof I am accused of the Jews:

3 Especially *because I know* thee to be expert in all customs and questions which are among the Jews: wherefore I beseech thee to hear me patiently.

4 My manner of life from my youth, which was at the first among mine own nation at Jerusalem, know all the Jews;

5 Which knew me from the beginning, if they would testify, that after the most straitest sect of our religion I lived a Pharisee.

6 And now I stand and am judged for the hope of the promise made of God unto our fathers:

7 Unto which *promise* our twelve tribes, instantly serving *God* day and night, hope to come. For which hope's sake, king Ā-grĭp′-pă, I am accused of the Jews.

8 Why should it be thought a thing incredible with you, that God should raise the dead?

9 I verily thought with myself, that I ought to do many things contrary to the name of Jesus of Nazareth.

10 Which thing I also did in Jerusalem: and many of the saints did I shut up in prison, having received authority from the chief priests; and when they were put to death, I gave my voice against *them.*

11 And I punished them oft in every synagogue, and compelled *them* to blaspheme; and being exceedingly mad against them, I persecuted *them* even unto strange cities.

12 Whereupon as I went to Damascus with authority and commission from the chief priests,

13 At midday, O king, I saw in the way a light from heaven, above the brightness of the sun, shining round about me and them which journeyed with me.

14 And when we were all fallen to the earth, I heard a voice speaking unto me, and saying in the Hebrew tongue, Saul, Saul, why persecutest thou me? *it is* hard for thee to kick against the pricks.

15 And I said, Who art thou, Lord? And he said, I am Jesus whom thou persecutest.

16 But rise, and stand upon thy feet: for I have appeared unto thee for this purpose, to make thee a minister and a witness both of these things which thou hast seen, and of those things in the which I will appear unto thee;

17 Delivering thee from the people, and *from* the Gentiles, unto whom now I send thee,

18 To open their eyes, *and* to turn *them* from darkness to light, and *from* the power of Satan unto God, that they may receive forgiveness of sins, and inheritance among them which are sanctified by faith that is in me.

19 Whereupon, O king Ā-grĭp′-pă, I was not disobedient unto the heavenly vision:

20 But shewed first unto them of Damascus, and at Jerusalem, and throughout all the coasts of Judæa, and *then* to the Gentiles, that they should repent and turn to God, and do works meet for repentance.

21 For these causes the Jews caught me in the temple, and went about to kill *me.*

22 Having therefore obtained help of God, I continue unto this day, witnessing both to small and great, saying none other things than those which the prophets and Moses did say should come:

23 That Christ should suffer, *and* that he should be the first that should rise from the dead, and should shew light unto the people, and to the Gentiles.

24 And as he thus spake for himself, Festus said with a loud voice, Paul, thou art beside thyself; much learning doth make thee mad.

25 But he said, I am not mad, most noble Festus; but speak forth the words of truth and soberness.

26 For the king knoweth of these things, before whom also I speak freely: for I am persuaded that

none of these things are hidden from him; for this thing was not done in a corner.

27 King Ă-grĭp′-pă, believest thou the prophets? I know that thou believest.

28 Then Ă-grĭp′-pă said unto Paul, Almost thou persuadest me to be a Christian.

29 And Paul said, I would to God, that not only thou, but also all that hear me this day, were both almost, and altogether such as I am, except these bonds.

30 And when he had thus spoken, the king rose up, and the governor, and Bĕr-nī′-çē, and they that sat with them:

31 And when they were gone aside, they talked between themselves, saying, This man doeth nothing worthy of death or of bonds.

32 Then said Ă-grĭp′-pă unto Festus, This man might have been set at liberty, if he had not appealed unto Cæsar.

These three chapters describe Paul's captivity in Caesarea. Was Paul distressed? To whom was he able to witness?

Compare the tactful tone of Paul's witness messages here with the approach he used in witnessing to:

the philosophers (17:22)
the religious Jews in the synagogue (13:16)

Which of the following groups of people would you find to be the most difficult to witness to? the least difficult?

| | |
|---|---|
| the rich | the politician |
| the military | the educated |
| the street person | the youth |
| the middle class | the aged |

Write out a personal witness to the group you listed as most difficult to witness to.

What can a twentieth-century witness learn from Paul's experiences of witnessing to wealthy politicians? How did his messages vary? List the similarities in each.

Compare the variety of responses to Paul's witness messages. Have you experienced similar reactions to your witness?

Were Paul's days spent in confinement at Caesarea wasted? How can witnesses today make witnessing opportunities out of confinements?

King Agrippa was very close to salvation. Can a person believe that Christ lived, died, arose, ascended, and not be saved? What is missing? What action, if any, should a witness take at that point?

## 23. WITNESSING IN ROME (27:1–28:31)

### CHAPTER 27

AND when it was determined that we should sail into Italy, they delivered Paul and certain other prisoners unto *one* named Julius, a centurion of Augustus' band.

2 And entering into a ship of Ăd-ră-mўt'-tĭ-ŭm, we launched, meaning to sail by the coasts of Asia; *one* Ăr-ĭs-tär'-chŭs, a Macedonian of Thĕss-ă-lō-nī'-că, being with us.

3 And the next *day* we touched at Sidon. And Julius courteously entreated Paul, and gave *him* liberty to go unto his friends to refresh himself.

4 And when we had launched from thence, we sailed under Cyprus, because the winds were contrary.

5 And when we had sailed over the sea of Çĭ-lĭç'-ĭ-ă and Pamphylia, we came to Myra, *a city* of Lўç'-ĭ-ă.

6 And there the centurion found a ship of Alexandria sailing into Italy; and he put us therein.

7 And when we had sailed slowly many days, and scarce were come over against Cnī'-dŭs, the wind not suffering us, we sailed under Crete, over against Săl-mō'-nē;

8 And, hardly passing it, came unto a place which is called The fair havens; nigh whereunto was the city *of* Lă-sē'-ă.

9 Now when much time was spent, and when sailing was now dangerous, because the fast was now already past, Paul admonished *them*,

10 And said unto them, Sirs, I perceive that this voyage will be with hurt and much damage, not only of the lading and ship, but also of our lives.

11 Nevertheless the centurion believed the master and the owner of the ship, more than those things which were spoken by Paul.

12 And because the haven was not commodious to winter in, the more part advised to depart thence also, if by any means they might attain to Phē-nī'-çē, *and there* to winter; *which is* an haven of Crete, and lieth toward the south-west and north-west.

13 And when the south wind blew softly, supposing that they had obtained *their* purpose, loos-

ing *thence*, they sailed close by Crete.

14 But not long after there arose against it a tempestuous wind, called Eû-rŏc′-lȳ-don.

15 And when the ship was caught, and could not bear up into the wind, we let *her* drive.

16 And running under a certain island which is called Clauda, we had much work to come by the boat:

17 Which when they had taken up, they used helps, undergirding the ship; and, fearing lest they should fall into the quicksands, strake sail, and so were driven.

18 And we being exceedingly tossed with a tempest, the next *day* they lightened the ship;

19 And the third *day* we cast out with our own hands the tackling of the ship.

20 And when neither sun nor stars in many days appeared, and no small tempest lay on *us*, all hope that we should be saved was then taken away.

21 But after long abstinence Paul stood forth in the midst of them, and said, Sirs, ye should have hearkened unto me, and not have loosed from Crete, and to have gained this harm and loss.

22 And now I exhort you to be of good cheer: for there shall be no loss of *any man's* life among you, but of the ship.

23 For there stood by me this night the angel of God, whose I am, and whom I serve,

24 Saying, Fear not, Paul; thou must be brought before Cæsar: and, lo, God hath given thee all them that sail with thee.

25 Wherefore, sirs, be of good cheer: for I believe God, that it shall be even as it was told me.

26 Howbeit we must be cast upon a certain island.

27 But when the fourteenth night was come, as we were driven up and down in Adria, about midnight the shipmen deemed that they drew near to some country;

28 And sounded, and found *it* twenty fathoms: and when they had gone a little further, they sounded again, and found *it* fifteen fathoms.

29 Then fearing lest we should have fallen upon rocks, they cast four anchors out of the stern, and wished for the day.

30 And as the shipmen were about to flee out of the ship, when they had let down the boat into the sea, under colour as though they would have cast anchors out of the foreship,

31 Paul said to the centurion and to the soldiers, Except these abide in the ship, ye cannot be saved.

32 Then the soldiers cut off the ropes of the boat, and let her fall off.

33 And while the day was coming on, Paul besought *them* all to take meat, saying, This day is the fourteenth day that ye have tarried and continued fasting, having taken nothing.

34 Wherefore I pray you to take *some* meat: for this is for your health: for there shall not an hair fall from the head of any of you.

35 And when he had thus spoken, he took bread, and gave thanks to God in presence of them all: and when he had broken *it*, he began to eat.

36 Then were they all of good cheer, and they also took *some* meat.

37 And we were in all in the ship two hundred threescore and sixteen souls.

38 And when they had eaten enough, they lightened the ship, and cast out the wheat into the sea.

39 And when it was day, they knew not the land: but they discovered a certain creek with a shore, into the which they were minded, if it were possible, to thrust in the ship.

40 And when they had taken up the anchors, they committed *themselves* unto the sea, and loosed the rudder bands, and hoisted up the mainsail to the wind, and made toward shore.

41 And falling into a place where two seas met, they ran the ship aground; and the forepart stuck fast, and remained unmoveable, but the hinder part was broken with the violence of the waves.

42 And the soldiers' counsel was

to kill the prisoners, lest any of them should swim out, and escape.

43 But the centurion, willing to save Paul, kept them from *their* purpose; and commanded that they which could swim should cast *themselves* first *into the sea,* and get to land:

44 And the rest, some on boards, and some on *broken pieces* of the ship. And so it came to pass, that they escaped all safe to land.

## CHAPTER 28

AND when they were escaped, then they knew that the island was called Melita.

2 And the barbarous people shewed us no little kindness: for they kindled a fire, and received us every one, because of the present rain, and because of the cold.

3 And when Paul had gathered a bundle of sticks, and laid *them* on the fire, there came a viper out of the heat, and fastened on his hand.

4 And when the barbarians saw the *venomous* beast hang on his hand, they said among themselves, No doubt this man is a murderer, whom, though he hath escaped the sea, yet vengeance suffereth not to live.

5 And he shook off the beast into the fire, and felt no harm.

6 Howbeit they looked when he should have swollen, or fallen down dead suddenly: but after they had looked a great while, and saw no harm come to him, they changed their minds, and said that he was a god.

7 In the same quarters were possessions of the chief man of the island, whose name was Publius; who received us, and lodged us three days courteously.

8 And it came to pass, that the father of Publius lay sick of a fever and of a bloody flux: to whom Paul entered in, and prayed, and laid his hands on him, and healed him.

9 So when this was done, others also, which had diseases in the island, came, and were healed:

10 Who also honoured us with many honours; and when we departed, they laded *us* with such things as were necessary.

11 And after three months we departed in a ship of Alexandria, which had wintered in the isle, whose sign was Castor and Pollux.

12 And landing at Sȳr′-ă-cūse, we tarried *there* three days.

13 And from thence we fetched a compass, and came to Rhē′-ġĭ-ŭm: and after one day the south wind blew, and we came the next day to Pū-tē′-ŏ-lī:

14 Where we found brethren, and were desired to tarry with them seven days: and so we went toward Rome.

15 And from thence, when the brethren heard of us, they came to meet us as far as Ăp′-pĭ-ī forum, and The three taverns: whom when Paul saw, he thanked God, and took courage.

16 And when we came to Rome, the centurion delivered the prisoners to the captain of the guard: but Paul was suffered to dwell by himself with a soldier that kept him.

17 And it came to pass, that after three days Paul called the chief of the Jews together: and when they were come together, he said unto them, Men *and* brethren, though I have committed nothing against the people, or customs of our fathers, yet was I delivered prisoner from Jerusalem into the hands of the Romans.

18 Who, when they had examined me, would have let *me* go, because there was no cause of death in me.

19 But when the Jews spake against *it,* I was constrained to appeal unto Cæsar; not that I had aught to accuse my nation of.

20 For this cause therefore have I called for you, to see *you,* and to speak with *you:* because that for the hope of Israel I am bound with this chain.

21 And they said unto him, We neither received letters out of Judæa concerning thee, neither any of the brethren that came shewed or spake any harm of thee.

22 But we desire to hear of thee what thou thinkest: for as concerning this sect, we know that every where it is spoken against.

23 And when they had appointed him a day, there came many to him into *his* lodging; to whom he expounded and testified the kingdom of God, persuading them concerning Jesus, both out of the law of Moses, and *out of* the prophets, from morning till evening.

24 And some believed the things which were spoken, and some believed not.

25 And when they agreed not among themselves, they departed, after that Paul had spoken one word, Well spake the Holy Ghost by Ē-sâi'-ăs the prophet unto our fathers,

26 Saying, Go unto this people, and say, Hearing ye shall hear, and shall not understand; and seeing ye shall see, and not perceive:

27 For the heart of this people is waxed gross, and their ears are dull of hearing, and their eyes have they closed; lest they should see with *their* eyes, and hear with *their* ears, and understand with *their* heart, and should be converted, and I should heal them.

28 Be it known therefore unto you, that the salvation of God is sent unto the Gentiles, and *that* they will hear it.

29 And when he had said these words, the Jews departed, and had great reasoning among themselves.

30 And Paul dwelt two whole years in his own hired house, and received all that came in unto him,

31 Preaching the kingdom of God, and teaching those things which concern the Lord Jesus Christ, with all confidence, no man forbidding him.

Compare Rome with Jerusalem. Why was Paul so anxious to witness in Rome? Why was it God's will for Paul to witness in Rome?

Why didn't God make it easy for Paul to get to Rome? Why doesn't God make easy witnessing opportunities today?

List the difficulties and trials that Paul experienced on the way to Rome. Was the Holy Spirit still guiding? Why is the leading of the Holy Spirit an important element in witnessing?

Notice how God supplied the needs of the witness (28:1-10).

Within the space of a month or two Paul testified to

dignitaries, to barbarians, to people in the capital of the world! How varied is your witness? Share your most exciting witnessing attempt.

When Paul arrived at Puteoli, he met brethren [fellow Christians] there. How could this be, since Paul had never witnessed there? Can we ever know the extent of our witness?

Paul accomplished more while he was in prison in Rome than most witnesses do outside of prison. Why weren't his witnessing days over?

How do the last words of the Book of Acts prove that the Holy Spirit was very much concerned with the witness of Christ? Show how His formula for witnessing is still working in chapter 28. Does that formula apply to witnesses today?

Take a moment now for a time of prayer, asking the expert on witnessing (the Holy Spirit), to fill you for His work.

## *THE MISSING WORD IN ACTS*

As you studied the Book of Acts, did you notice that a word was missing? It's one of our most commonly used words, a word that song writers seldom leave out of a new song. The word is exhaustless in meaning, yet it is often misused. The word is *love.*

The word *love* appears in twenty-seven books of the Old Testament and in twenty-one books of the New Testament. Why didn't the writer of Acts use it?

The best personification of love is God. First Corinthians 13 is often called the love chapter. The Book of Acts illustrates love in action.

### LOVE IS PATIENT

The early witnesses waited for the Holy Spirit and with dogged determination fulfilled the task their Savior asked of them.

### LOVE IS KIND

The Christians in Acts shared everything they had. No one claimed that any of his own possessions was his own. They served one another.

### LOVE DOES NOT ENVY

People outside the church envied the power of the Holy Spirit in the witnesses' lives. But the Christians esteemed others better than themselves.

## LOVE DOES NOT BOAST

The only thing the witness boasted of was the resurrected Lord.

## LOVE IS NOT PROUD

They counted themselves as dung and their lives as nothing for the Gospel's sake.

## LOVE IS NOT RUDE

The witnesses preached with neither fear or favor but always with tact.

## LOVE IS NOT SELF-SEEKING

Several times men were ready to worship the witnesses. But the witnesses always stopped such worship. No one witness demanded the leadership.

## LOVE IS NOT EASILY ANGERED

Anger was shown many times by the enemies of the witnesses but only seldom by the witnesses.

## LOVE KEEPS NO RECORD OF WRONG

The early Christians were grossly mistreated, but never evened the score. They were persecuted unto death but only forgave.

## LOVE DOES NOT DELIGHT IN EVIL BUT REJOICES IN THE TRUTH

Much joy is expressed throughout Acts. Why? Their Lord was raised from the dead!

## LOVE ALWAYS PROTECTS

The early church gathered together not only for fellowship, but also because there was strength in numbers.

## LOVE ALWAYS TRUSTS

Believers in Acts trusted the Savior, trusted each other, trusted the truth of the Gospel, trusted God's Word.

## LOVE ALWAYS HOPES

For the hope that was within them, the witnesses in Acts were always ready to give the answer.

## LOVE ALWAYS PERSEVERES

They witnessed at the cost of leaving their homes and belongings. They persevered in their duty even though beaten, threatened, imprisoned, and shipwrecked—even murdered—for the Gospel's sake.

## LOVE NEVER FAILS

The early Christians in Acts only found three things that last and will not fade away. These are faith, hope, and love. "The greatest of these is love."

The pattern is clear.
The call to action has been sounded.
Go out, twentieth-century witness,
and tell the GOOD NEWS!